When the Summer Ended

One Woman's War Story

When the Summer Ended

*by Cecylia Wolkowinska
and Joanna Bogle*

GRACEWING
LEOMINSTER

First Published in 1992

Gracewing
Fowler Wright Books
Southern Ave, Leominster
Herefordshire HR6 0QF

Gracewing Books are distributed

In New Zealand by
Catholic Supplies Ltd
80 Adelaide Rd
Wellington
New Zealand

In Australia by
Charles Paine Pty
8 Ferris Street
North Parramatta
NSW 2151 Australia

In Canada by
Novails
P.O. Box 990
Outremont H2V 457
Canada

In USA by
Morehouse Publishing
P.O. Box 1321
Harrisburg
PA 17105
U.S.A.

Typesetting by Action Typesetting Limited, Gloucester

Printed and bound in Great Britain by
Dotesios, Trowbridge, Wilts

ISBN 0 85244 216 5

To the memory of my parents
Pamięci moich Rodziców Poświęcom

C. W

Authors Notes

I met Cecylia Wolkowinska through our joint interest in the work of Aid to the Church in Need, a Catholic charity specialising in giving help to Eastern Europe. When I learned that, during World War II, she had been a member of the Polish Underground and had fought in the Warsaw Rising, I was naturally intrigued. She first told me the outline of her story in 1985, under some pressure from me, as I was seeking information for a South London newspaper as part of a feature article commemorating the 40th anniversary of the ending of the war. For me it opened up a new dimension of history. I realised that I was hearing, for the first time, the full story of a typical member of Britain's large Polish community. I had somehow always taken the presence of this community for granted. Growing up in Britain in the 1960s, I had known girls at school who had Polish surnames and whose parents spoke with foreign accents. I knew that the presence of such families in Britain related to the war and its aftermath, but never understood exactly why they were here and not in Poland. I think it is important that the story of this Polish community is known and understood − not only because it is a brave and exciting tale but because it fills the gaps in the standard British view of World War II.

Working on this book was a fascinating experience for me, but a much harder one for Cecylia, who had to relive so many tragic events and revive sad memories. I have learned a great deal and am grateful for having had this unique opportunity of learning history at first hand.

Joanna Bogle
London, 1992

On both sides of my family, generation after generation fought for the independence of Poland and endured imprisonment, hardship, and exile for the cause.

Our generation inherited a free and independent Poland — but we were only allowed to have it for twenty years. Poland then faced an attack perhaps more savage than any in its history. Many years later, after the fighting was over and I had settled in England, friends urged me to tell the story — because it was not just the story of my own experiences but was typical of all the Poles of the Home Army who ended up as exiles. I only finally embarked upon the tale, however, because I was persuaded that it might be a useful addition to other accounts, and give a personal description from the point of view of one very ordinary Polish girl caught up in great events. Many other people — especially from the eastern part of Poland — had more tragic and terrible experiences. Each account helps to explain the full story of what happened to our country.

The story here is written in English so that people in Britain, North America and elsewhere can read it, and thus start to understand about the Polish community living amongst them. I could not have done it without Joanna Bogle, whose enthusiasm and determination ensured that we overcame the problems of language, and whose commitment made me carry on when I would sometimes rather have given up!

I dedicate this story to my sons, daughters-in-law, and grandchildren, now living in France, Britain and Australia, so that they can know about their Polish heritage. I also dedicate it to the honoured memory of my parents.

Cecylia Wolkowinska

Chapter One

It was an unbelievably beautiful summer. As I lay on my back in the orchard, the trees bent their loaded branches down towards me. Heavy with their fruit, they seemed to beckon me to climb up and pick an apple or a pear. The scene of ripeness filled the air. Above the trees the sky was wide and blue to the horizon. Insects buzzed about. High up a single bird flew by. The trees rustled a little with the faintest of breezes. In the heavy heat the essence of the afternoon was a deep and serene silence.

Here in the heart of the countryside no roar of traffic disturbed the calm and no petrol fumes tainted the air. We clip-clopped to church on Sundays in a carriage drawn by a pair of horses along the dusty roads. The country folk disdained shoes and walked barefoot, pausing to relax and enjoy the coolness of the water at every river or stream. This was timeless, changeless rural Poland, with its rhythm of work and rest, evening music and Sunday Mass, golden harvest and tables spread with traditional fare.

That summer seemed to have a quality all its own, different from any other that I could remember. As the corn ripened in a glory of gold and the sun poured out its heat day after day, it seemed as if the very earth was breathing, panting with the heavy breath of summer.

The earth was warm and breathing beneath me now as I lay looking up at the trees. My books were scattered around me — I had plenty of studying to do, with the new academic year starting in September and matriculation looming. But the wider world seemed very remote here in the dozing peace

1

of the countryside. I savoured these summer hours — lessons could wait.

The summer had been a special one in many ways. I was at the end of my teens, and had just completed my first year of lycée, specialising in the humanities — French, Latin, history, Polish literature — and living in rooms in Warsaw. With the start of the long summer holidays I had paid my landlady, packed my bags, and departed for the Tatra mountains where I was due to take part in a course for girls run by the Sodality of the Virgin Mary. The *Sodalicja Mariańska* was a popular movement in Poland and played a big part in many people's lives. It ran religious education courses as well as various other activities for different age groups.

Music, talks and outings around the countryside made up a busy programme. I was almost sorry when I had to leave the course a couple of days early to return to Warsaw for an important family event — my brother's wedding. Janek and Helena were married at the Wizytki Church, which was very popular for weddings. They had what was called a 'Roman wedding', meaning a morning one with a full Nuptial Mass, as opposed to the alternative of an evening ceremony without Mass. Helena wore a smart white day-dress with a fur wrap and carried a beautiful bouquet. My mother looked elegant in a splendid hat with ostrich feathers. There was a reception in a smart restaurant, with the bride and groom being greeted with the traditional gifts of bread and salt, and then toasts and speeches at the end of the meal as we lingered over coffee, cognac, and gateaux.

I was very much the youngest of the family. My three older sisters were all now married with families of their own. The eldest, Jadwiga, and her husband Edek had a baby daughter. They had moved away from Warsaw for a while but Edek's job was bringing them back to the city and they were planning to return. Meanwhile, however, Jadwiga and the little girl were planning to spend most of the hottest weeks of the summer out in the countryside. Zofia and her husband Edzio and their five children lived over in the south-west of Poland, in Silesia close to the German border. Wanda and her doctor husband Bronek lived near Lodz. They had one little boy, Bolek my godson, and Wanda was expecting a second child.

My mother – my father had died when I was a baby and I had no memories of him at all – had spent the past few years living with one or other of my married sisters. I lived in digs in Warsaw. I sometimes chafed against being treated so very obviously as the junior member of the family unit, and I disliked not having a settled home. Yet the city of Warsaw was a place where I had a great sense of belonging. My mother knew it very well and had passed on to all her children a genuine affection for it. Warsaw had an atmosphere all its own, different from Krakow or Poznan. It was a more international city. Like Vienna or Paris, it had innumerable hotels and cafes, where people met to socialise over coffee while music played: the talk would go back and forth while one sipped a capuchino or a black coffee, or toyed with a slice of cake and watched the world go by.

Our family tradition was one of strong Polish patriotism. In the first years of the century, when Poland was still divided up between the Russian, Prussian, and Austrian empires, my father had been arrested for his patriotic activities while he was still a young medical student. He was taken by the Russians to Siberia, for forced labour in the gold-mines, and was to bear the marks of the chains on his wrists all his life. When he was released he was banned from the territories ruled by the Russians and went to Krakow, then under Austrian rule. Here he started his medical studies again from scratch, qualified, and worked as a doctor. Later when he met my mother they settled on a family estate which she had inherited in the east of Poland, where he put his medical skills at the service of the local population. Here, my brother and sisters were born. But during the 1917 Revolution the family had to flee, settled once again in Krakow, where I was born. When my mother was widowed, she came to Warsaw to make her home with her married daughters.

Central to our family life was the Christian faith, with its magnificent truths and rock-solid principles for living. We had had our difficult times – money was short when I was growing up – but this faith, for my mother and all of us, was a real source of strength and inspiration.

The next major step in my life was going to be matriculation, and after that university. Plans for this were still at the discussion stage, but one idea that I had talked over with my headmistress was that I might go abroad — to Belgium or to France. Life seemed to be opening up in so many exciting ways, and I was thinking of studying the social sciences, or maybe following in my father's footsteps and becoming a doctor. My family situation had encouraged me to be independent, and to think ahead, and to recognise the importance of serving the country in some way.

Summer in Warsaw, like summer in any big city, could be hot, sticky, and unpleasant. I was delighted when one of my teachers, who had taken a particular interest in me and my work, asked me if I would like to go with her and her husband when they went down to the country for a few weeks. They would be staying with friends whose home was an old manor-house some way north-east of Warsaw. This was an unexpected bonus, and after Janek's wedding I gratefully accepted the invitation and found myself a guest in an old-style Polish country house, Hornostajewicze, not far from Grodno.

My hosts were much older than me, and I was a little shy at first. But this soon disappeared in the warm welcome. Everyone was very kind and I was treated like one of the family, with my own room and an invitation to spend each day as I chose.

My favourite spot was the orchard, where I would go after breakfast every day, ostensibly to study but really to read and dream and muse. The summer days stretched long and golden ahead, and there was a deep sense of relaxation. Lying here, I was in the heart of rural Poland, deep within Europe, miles from any coast. To the east lay the Soviet Union, a nation that had proved itself no friend of the independent nation of Poland. Poland's traditional way of life was based upon farms and farm-owning families.

We had always looked westwards towards France and to Rome for our cultural links. We had a profound sense of being European as well as Slavonic. Far to the west lay Germany. She too had often proved herself to be our enemy and had ruled over large areas of Polish territory.

Poland had achieved her independence in 1918, under the Treaty of Versailles which ended the First World War. Then had come the attempt by the Bolsheviks from Russia to invade Poland – Lenin's dream had been to conquer the whole of Europe for the new communist creed. Halted on the banks of the Vistula by the fledgeling Polish army, they were turned back, and Poles spoke of the 'cud nad Vistula' – the 'miracle on the Vistula' in 1920 which had saved not only our nation but the whole continent from Communist rule.

Now, only twenty years later, there were new pressures on the treaty settlement. The map of Europe that had been drawn at Versailles had created new resentments. Some of its territorial division seemed arbitrary. In Germany there were plenty of voices calling for change and these enabled the Nazi party to sweep all before it and to threaten our peace and stability.

I knew that in the background, hidden in the summer's heartbeat, there was a growing tension. During the long sunny hours one could avoid it, but as the afternoon stretched on to evening, and everyone gathered at the house to eat and talk, its haunting presence was all too obvious. The radio became the focal point of all our evenings, and we would all be silent and tense as it was switched on for the News.

Of course everyone had known for a long while about Germany's attitude towards Poland, and Hitler's designs on the country and the threats and provocations that he made. All Poles knew – had always known – just how vulnerable our country was, and how precarious was our hard-won independence. There was a real threat of invasion. The silence and peace of the orchard was deceptive, and in our hearts we all knew it. Back in March my brother-in-law Bronek, who as a doctor served in the Army reserve, had been formally mobilised. There was no point in having any false illusions about why this was considered necessary.

Service in the reserves was compulsory for Poland's young men, and there were various different categories of involvement. For those who had passed matriculation there was a special status which committed them to accept particular responsibilities as being potential officers. Boys knew all about the system as they were growing up because there were cadet units in schools with training in drill and basic military principles. We girls also had training in things like First Aid. Bronek's mobilisation had meant that instead of being merely available on an official list he was now active and had been sent to join a unit based somewhere along our long vulnerable border with Germany.

These reserve officers were really the best of our nation: the lawyers and teachers, university professors, businessmen, writers and engineers, all willing to serve and protect their country when the need arose.

Young people brought up in the new independent Polish nation were fiercely proud of its achievements. We were taught in school and at home how in just a few years the country had welded together an independent judicial system with a unified structure of courts and judges, a credible political system with a means of formulating laws, and a common system of schools and universities and higher education. Industrialisation of our hitherto rural-based economy had also been begun. There was a tremendous sense of excitement, genuine achievement which communicated itself to young people and which formed the atmosphere in which we were being reared.

For such young people, it was unthinkable that Poland would ever be crushed again. We were taught history with an eye to the present. There was a stress on a sense of responsibility towards the nation. The idea of a thriving democracy was promoted in schools where every class had its class president, and there were committees and organisations for different activities. Outside school the Guides and Scouts were popular, promoting ideas of teamwork and service with a commitment to a threefold ideal of 'country, knowledge and virtue': 'Ojczyzna – Nauka – Cnota'.

I was a class president – later school president – and always very active in whatever was going on. Our class committees took on serious responsibilities: we raised money for needy families and arranged to visit and befriend them, and we organised a system in which pupils who were good in particular subjects coached the less able.

When I look back, many years later, those last golden weeks of peace in August 1939 have a special glow, a peculiar beauty and mood. They have lingered in my memory as a dreamlike, unique time with the scent and the flavour and the charm of old rural Poland around them. It's almost as if that summer was a gift, something to treasure and remember for always: the very essence, somehow, of all the old times. I could not know just how swiftly and how tragically these times were going to change.

Chapter Two

As family and guests gathered round the radio in the old manor-house that evening, faces were tense and solemn. The news had been sinister for days. The radio was broadcasting reports on what had initially been our army's routine summer exercises. Suddenly this emphasis on military manoeuvres had an all too obvious significance. The news reports also told us about our Foreign Minister coming and going in meetings with the French and British governments, and with the German government. Everyone knew that soon, perhaps very soon, our nation could be at war.

Despite the growing realisation of what was coming, ordinary people were left in a quandary over what to do. For young people like me, war was something quite unknown. We couldn't envisage it at all. The older generation remembered the First World War, when there had been fighting on and around Polish territory. Poles had been called up to the different armies – Poland being at that time divided up between Russia, Prussia, and Austria – and the families of those who fought settled down to cope as best they could. Their horses and crops were commandeered, their farms and livelihoods threatened, but they stayed in their own homes and struggled on. That was what the word 'war' conjured up. No one could have envisaged the war that was to come.

We all thought that here, in the eastern province of Poland, miles from the German border, there seemed a good measure of safety. We would be a good long way from the fighting. Surely no invasion force would penetrate as far as this.

My one thought at this time was to get back to my

own family, to face whatever might happen with them. In any crisis such as this, one's natural reaction was to head for home.

'I've got to get back to Warsaw. If I don't go now, the route might be cut off. If there's going to be an invasion . . .' None of us really knew what sort of scenario to expect and we were all simply trying to apply our common sense to the immediate problems.

My teacher and her husband who like me were guests and were torn in their minds between this rural manor-house and their own home base in Warsaw, took a different view of things from me. They felt that from the purely practical point of view the safest place to be was here in the countryside. Warsaw was the capital − a place of trouble and tension and the focus for everything that was going on. A train journey in any case posed unnecessary risks. Surely it was better to wait in the known safety of a rural backwater than to risk what might be a prolonged zigzag trip across to the capital city, while the nation was mobilising and a vast enemy roared its readiness on the frontier?

The talk went to and fro, weighing up this argument and that, speculating, worrying, tossing different decisions about. But I was certain that Warsaw was where I ought to be, and my host family accepted my decision as one that I must, in the final analysis, make for myself.

What I could not know then was that this was a decision which was to spare me the fate that would bear down on them just a short while later.

The next day was a scramble of packing, of goodbyes to the people who had been so kind to me, of warm thanks for good times, of hastily-packed picnic meals, and hugs and wishes of mutual good fortune in whatever was to come.

The railway station was a crush of confusion and noise, and the train, when it came in, like none I had ever seen. Every corner of it was crammed with soldiers, all being rushed westwards, and all talking, being ordered about, seeking news, eager, energetic and excited. Everyone was speculating over what was about to happen. The chatter and shouting was tremendous and overwhelming. I managed to jam myself aboard. I seemed to be the only civilian in the teeming mass — and the only female! The young soldiers in my carriage joked and flirted with me — to have a girl to whom they could chatter and brag just about crowned their excitement. The atmosphere was bubbling with optimism and vigour — 'We'll show those Germans!' — and I was caught up in it. But I was also nervous and taut inside. My thoughts raced ahead to Warsaw, to my mother and the rest of my family, hoping that they were all right. Everything seemed to be happening so fast.

It was August 30th: the harvest in the fields was mostly already gathered and stacked, and the stubble stretched golden to the horizon. Here and there some fields of sugar-beet still awaited picking. The train was stuffy and airless, packed with young Poles of all types. Above, the sky was still a brilliant blue and the sun burned down on the countryside. In many places the soil had been baked so hard that it had great straggling cracks in it.

The soldiers laughed and talked in loud voices, tried to draw me into conversation, and offered me cigarettes. My worry about getting safely home took the edge off my ability to share in their mood of cheerful determination.

I arrived in a Warsaw that was steeling itself for the inevitable. It was in fact just 36 hours away from war. When I look back now I can remember the tension, the fever of military activity, the desperate search for reliable information.

I hurried to the flat where Janek and Helena had set up home just a month before, after their wedding.

'Mamusia!' It was good to see my mother there and to know that the family unit was collecting itself together. As we hugged the news poured out. People in Warsaw were better informed than we had been down in the countryside: no one was in any doubt about the fact that Germany was going to invade, that Poland would fight back, and that the battle was going to be a bitter one. The one hope lay in strong allies. Would Britain and France — both of which had agreed to stand by Poland in the event of any aggression — prove to be steadfast allies?

'I'll be getting my mobilisation papers any day now', said Janek. 'Did you see all the posters everywhere?' I had been greeted by these at the station: placards calling on men from various age-groups to report to the specified Army centres as soon as they received their papers. The machinery which alerted the nation's armed forces had swung into action.

Helena prepared supper for us — it went without saying that I would stay with them for as long as it took to find out what was going to happen next. 'What about Jadzia — down in the country? Have you heard anything?' The invasion was catching thousands of Polish families in the same situation, split up in different places because of the summer holidays. It seemed that every able bodied person was on the move.

The priority in Warsaw was to collect together tinned food and other emergency supplies. Special sticky paper had suddenly appeared in the shops, to paste over windows so that the glass would not be thrown everywhere when they shattered in the blasts of a bombing raid. People were terrified of gas. Rumours about different deadly weapons were circulating, and there were a thousand grisly scenarios of what might happen.

In Janek and Helena's flat, the remains of their very recent wedding lent an air of unreality to what was going on. Bottles of wines and spirits left from the reception were still stacked in the cupboard, these jostled with the goods they had collected as part of their war preparations such as tinned sardines. How was it possible to be so afraid and apprehensive when only recently we had all been celebrating together?

In the early hours of Friday 1st September, Germany invaded Poland. We were quickly made aware of this with a steady thundering roar which roused us from our beds and set the walls and roofs shaking. A ferocious pounding of our city had begun. This was 'blitzkrieg', an annihilating, shattering, lightning-speed invasion which swept away cities and communities which lay in its path, wrecking any pre-lanned schemes for defence and protection and tossing humanity before it like leaves into a bonfire.

The radio warned of a coming air-raid and then out in the streets the sirens crackled into action and people ran, sometimes wearing only odd bits of clothing, sometimes

screaming, sometimes carrying a few precious family oddments, into the shelters which had been hastily formed from
the basements, cellars, sheds and the sturdier parts of major
buildings. Air-raid workers were on hand to shepherd people
to appointed places and to take charge and avoid panic. The
planes above us were Stukas, as we later discovered. They
seemed to dive straight down towards us, sending out an
appalling screaming noise. As they arrived they throbbed
overhead and then would add to the din of Warsaw as one
section of the city after another received their bombs. The
massive air bombardment that was to reduce so much of the
city to ruins over the next few days had begun in a style
which was to become sickeningly familiar.

The hot summer weather, which had seemed so glorious
only days before, was now suddenly menacing and merciless.
'Why doesn't it rain? Why can't we get some cover from
the clouds?' The clear skies offered the invading bombers
the magnificent vision they wanted. Tiny fighter planes of
the Polish air force going up to struggle against them had
nowhere to hide.

When the bombs weren't actually falling, people gathered
in huddles in the streets to scan the skies, their arms sheltering
their faces from the fierce glare of the sun, watching the
dog-fights as the aeroplanes circled and swooped in the
pitiless blue. Sometimes a German machine caught fire and
circled, spinning downwards, with red flames and a widening
spiral of thick black smoke pouring from its rear. A great
roaring cheer then went up from the watchers below. But
this was only one plane – and a great many of our own
Polish fighter-pilots were going down too. We were to gather
to watch these dog fights again and again over the next few
days, always cheering on our side and willing them to victory.
But our air force had very few planes – and the Germans
had already bombed the airfields where they had been kept.
The odds were hopelessly against us.

When night fell it brought no relief. The stars glittered out
from a sky of sharpened clarity, and the bombers renewed
their attacks. Saturday saw the battle surging anew.

On Sunday morning, Janek received his *Karta
Mobilizacyjna*, and Mother, Helena and I went with

him to the station to see him off to war. It was packed. Men, some in uniform and some still in civilian clothes, were all saying goodbye to their families. As she did at the beginning of any journey or new undertaking, Mother traced the Sign of the Cross on Janek's forehead with her thumb in the traditional Polish way of invoking a blessing for what lay ahead. As we hugged him, we couldn't put our feelings properly into words. It was hardest on Helena — bride of only a month.

There was still no news of anyone else in the family. Jadwiga was, as far as any of us knew, still somewhere down in the countryside, and probably alone as Edek was in the reserves and had been immediately mobilised when tension began building up in the preceding weeks. Bronek, mobilised back in the spring, would be somewhere far to the west where the land fighting was taking place — as a doctor his place was with the men as they went into battle. Zofia and Edzio lived furthest west of all, in Silesia right up on the German border — were they fleeing to Warsaw with other refugees? Would they reach us?

Warsaw was embattled, but it was still very much Poland's capital. Restaurants and cafés were packed with people snatching a quick meal: officers, newspapermen, worried-looking family groups. The streets were full — men were anxiously sorting out mobilisation arrangements, collecting supplies, trying to get news. Everyone had his or her own particular worries and responsibilities, set against the general background horror of these first terrifying hours and days of war. Within a very short while, any semblance of normality in the way of shops and restaurants was to vanish.

It was after leaving the station that my mother and I heard the great news which was to send a crowd, of which we became part, pouring through the streets with a sudden zest and hope. It had been announced that morning that Britain and France, were after all coming to Poland's aid. They had stuck by their commitments to us, and they declared war on Germany.

Sweeping the city, the news created a great surge of life. Fresh hope sprang up everywhere. Gathering new people every moment, a crowd swept down towards Aleje

Ujazdowski, a parade of elegant houses opposite one of Warsaw's main parks. Here, flying the Union Jack and the Tricolour, stood the British and French embassies, impressive villas in lovely gardens.

How we shouted and cheered! We sang the French national anthem again and again. There had been strong bonds between Poland and France for centuries. We couldn't oblige with the British national anthem, as none of us knew the tune, but we could and did cheer Britain's name, and call out our gratitude and exult in our new-found thrill at knowing that Poland was not alone and that her allies had stood by her, as they had promised. The sickening horror of an overwhelming invasion from Germany began to recede, and in its place came the image of hundreds of aeroplanes speeding to our aid, armed and equipped for war, teaming up with our Polish fighters to turn the Germans away in battle after battle. Britain, with her massive worldwide empire, was surely a force to be reckoned with – and France, our friend for so long, was a nation we could trust.

We felt that help was truly on the way. Emotion swept the crowd as a figure emerged from an embassy building to acknowledge our cheers with a wave and an awkward bowing and nodding. For us, it was as if the sound of planes from Britain's Royal Air Force, and the marching thud of French infantrymen's feet, could already be heard in the west. It was some while before the crowd finally dispersed and people made their way home to face another night of bombing in the surer hope of final victory. How bitterly disappointed we were all shortly to be over our allies – but we had no way of knowing that at this early stage.

Meanwhile the sky glowed red that night as the Germans returned to the attack and many of Warsaw's buildings crackled and burned in a terrifying inferno. The planes were now tearing the city apart with incendiary bombs, and the flames leapt up to destroy homes, schools, hospitals and churches.

Chapter Three

It had all seemed so simple and straightforward to an idealistic schoolgirl cheering outside a foreign embassy, but the realities of the next few weeks of the war were to prove very different. We waited in vain for any sign from the British or the French that they were at war. Eventually we did hear that they were sending aeroplanes to fly over Germany – but only to drop leaflets! We could hardly believe it. What could leaflets do when our towns and villages were burning?

'What do they think they're doing – dropping bits of paper while we're being invaded?' I and all my friends were shrill with indignation. It was only much later that we were to discover the grim truth – that Britain was wholly incapable of giving any practical aid to Poland. She did not have the right sort of aeroplanes, or anything like enough of them, and was hopelessly ill-prepared for a war involving an embattled nation deep in the heart of Europe. Poland must fight alone. On September 3rd the German Army was in fact already in Warsaw's suburbs: by the 11th the city was fully surrounded.

Much later I discovered that the next few weeks were being referred to in England as the 'phoney war'. It was anything but phoney to us in Warsaw. In the initial days of the fighting there was some semblance of normal life. A very few shops managed to stay open, although they had run out of anything anyone wanted. However, the sight of open shops was good for morale, a visible reminder of how life had been before. Some – not many – trams were running, and there was movement on the streets. However, as the Germans drew ever nearer, until eventually they had surrounded the city,

the fighting took on a new dimension. We were under siege.
Civil defence was organised and barricades went up in the
streets. A grim but determined spirit emerged.

At first, the main thrust of the battle centred on air raids.
Everyone quickly developed a pattern for these. They generally came at dawn, although there were also daytime raids.
The Germans, with their passion for systematic efficiency,
bombed us at set hours: at dawn, midday, and evening. The
warning would come through loudspeakers into every street:
'Attention! Attention! It's coming!' No one needed to ask
what 'it' was. Then the siren would wail. Mother would
immediately grab her three most treasured possessions – her
handbag, a travelling clock in a leather case, and a picture of
the Virgin Mary which had belonged to her parents, and had
come with her from the family estate in Podole in south-east
Poland in 1917. These would always, without fail, go with
her to the nearest shelter. The treasured picture eventually
survived not only this first Warsaw battle but also the almost
wholesale destruction of the city in the later Rising, and was
to find a home many years later in a different country, the
serene eyes of the Virgin gazing down on my children and
grandchildren from the wall of a London flat.

We took a big mattress down to the cellar and the three
of us, Mother, Helena and I, sat on it while destruction
hurtled down from the skies. During one particularly bad
raid, as I sat leaning against the wall, I felt it *move* behind
me. Immediately we all looked up to the ceiling: would it
hold? It did, and we survived for another day.

Every day, Mother and I would go out into the city to see
what was happening. We would go to Mass, check on the
whereabouts of friends, try to buy some food if there was
any available. On hearing the first air-raid siren, we would
dash for the nearest shelter, usually a cellar or the entrance to
a big block of flats. More than once, on passing the same spot
the next day, we saw that our temporary shelter had fallen
victim to a later raid and was a heap of smoking rubble.

The weather continued to be searingly hot. The only
protection from the sun came from the thick dust that now
formed a film over streets and buildings and had become a
part of existence in embattled Warsaw.

Hysteria hovered just beneath the surface. On one occasion a woman rushed in to the crowded and stuffy air-raid shelter shrieking with horror: in the confusion of the raid she had become separated from her child. Her terror was like a match dropped into dry tinder — within moments a great rush of fear was sweeping the crowd. I found myself doing something I had never done before — leaping up on to a table I shouted at everyone to stop it, to be quiet. To my horror I discovered I was using the sort of language a well brought up young woman would never normally use. Perhaps it was the shock value of this that produced the desired effect. The rush of panic was momentarily checked.

There was spy mania everywhere. Everyone seemed to have heard of a man in the next block who had been seen giving secret signals to the Germans to enable them to target their raids more accurately, or who was a saboteur hindering our defence efforts.

Now the battle changed and intensified. The enemy was attacking not only from the air but from every direction on land. We were under artillery fire. It was no longer possible to leave your place of shelter and search for food or friends. The German tanks rolled forward, cutting off the neighbouring villages and the surrounding countryside, isolating the capital. Somewhere in that desperate struggle around the city's outskirts Janek was fighting with his unit. We had no way of knowing whether he was still alive or had been killed or wounded.

Food began to run out as no supplies could reach us. One by one the various routes of access were sealed off. With the continuous air raids a stench of death — an unmistakable, sickening smell — began to pervade the streets. Bodies of dogs and horses and human beings lay unburied, rotting in the fierce heat, under the rubble of so many shattered houses — there was no time to dig them out and deal with them properly.

Jammed into a crowded shelter with strangers, Warsaw's citizens would await the crashes and roaring that spelt out the destruction of a building above their heads or further down the street — somebody's home, somebody's precious belongings and memories, somebody's livelihood. Emerging into the thick dust and smoke to pick their way home as best they could, their thoughts alternated between wondering if their own home was still there and speculating on how long they had got until the next raid.

A less significant irritation was the propaganda barrage from the Germans. Several times the city was showered with leaflets calling on us all to give up the fight, to admit the complete impossibility of holding out any longer and concede the German victory. These seemed curiously irrelevant – having lasted thus far, we would stick it out for as long as we could. Some people even still claimed that the British might be on their way.

Bread was running out. Queues stretched down streets, haunted by the constant nauseating stench. Back in the flat where Janek and Helena had so happily and hopefully set up home just a few weeks before, the little luxuries left over from the wedding added zest to the tinned sardines that formed our main food.

News seemed almost as vital as nourishment. No one knew exactly what was going on. Rumours flew around – about the government, about who exactly was in charge, about the British and the French, about what was going to happen next.[1] It was impossible to know whom to trust. Trenches were dug around the city to stop the German tanks – a call had gone out for all able-bodied men to help.

And now a fresh horror dawned. Across Poland's eastern frontiers, pounding the countryside, hard-baked under the unrelenting sun and as easy to ride on as a tarmac road surface, poured the tanks and guns and infantry of the Soviet Union's Red Army. It was September 17th, and the USSR, faithful to the secret Molotov/Ribbentrop agreement between the Soviet Union and Germany, was appropriating the Eastern provinces of our country and absorbing them behind its own borders.[2]

At first, news of this produced confusion and doubt. We had, of course, no knowledge about secret pacts between the German and Russian dictators at the time. What were the Soviets doing? Few Poles trusted them – indeed many had always seen them as a greater foe than the Germans. Later this eastern invasion was to become known as the 'stab in the back', and to be fully understood as playing a major part in forging Poland's tragic future. But in the first few days little was known about what was really going on.

Much later a picture emerged of what took place. Peaceful farms which had seemed so safe, remote from the ferocious fighting in the west, awoke to the noise of boots and marching, to rattling on doors and orders to 'open up'. The Soviets hauled bewildered people from their homes and forced them into cattle trucks which rolled eastwards into the USSR, without food or adequate water. Many died on the way of starvation and thirst. More died after arrival in the filth and horror of the labour camps. Many would never return — they would endure years of enforced settlement in the USSR, in camps and colonies. Some would eventually find their way out after fighting broke out between Germany and the USSR in 1941, and the Poles were formed into an Army to join in the battle. Others were prevented from reaching the recruitment centres. Thousands lingered in the remote regions of the Soviet Empire for years. Much careful research work in the confusion and uncertainty of a post-war Europe where Stalin cast his grim shadow would fail to reunite many tragically divided families. For so many people September 17th meant a sealing off from parents, spouses and children — people just vanished into the darkness of the Soviet Union and were never heard of again.

What had happened to the family at Hornostajewicze, where I had been staying just three weeks before? When news of the September 17th coup reached us, in Warsaw, my thoughts flew to the kindly old couple in the old manor house, with its golden fields and its fruited orchard, and its serene and unhurried way of life.

I have never been able to discover what happened to them, or to my teacher and her husband — Warsaw people like myself. Had I not taken that last train to Warsaw, hours before war broke out, I would have shared their fate, whatever it was. As 'landowners' my hosts would have belonged to the class of people most hated by the Soviets and the veil of silence thrown over them and their friends and neighbours is ominous. Forty years on, it remains impenetrable.[3] I can still recall that teacher's face, and remember that her Christian name was Janina, although as her pupil naturally I didn't call her that − I always addressed her formally as 'Madame'.

In Warsaw many men were to be caught up in the 'stab in the back' too. Shortly before the Soviet invasion, a radio broadcast insisted that men of all ages should flee the city and head away from the advancing Germans, eastwards out into the surrounding countryside. Many who followed this instruction after much heart-searching and some tragic farewells with their families found that they were heading straight into the grip of the USSR's army − and into imprisonment. This was a tragedy for Warsaw as we needed every possible man for our defence against the Germans. There is still controversy over this radio broadcast and over the motives of Umiastowski, the man who made it. Was it a genuine attempt to save crucial lives, which went hopelessly wrong? Or was there something more sinister behind it? In the atmosphere of the time, with accusations and counter-accusations of spying and treachery, it was difficult to know whom to trust.

The Polish Army was also to suffer from the Soviet invasion, and in a way that was to have searing, long-lasting effects. By September 17th, many regiments which had been fighting on the Western Front against the Germans had been forced back across the country, trying desperately to regroup to fight again. They were caught up in the Soviet sphere, and taken prisoner after a brief battle against hopeless odds. Later some families were to hear news of lost fathers and brothers and fiancés and were even able to exchange letters with them while they were in Soviet captivity. Then the letters stopped in the early months of 1940. Their tragic fate is worth noting here, although we did not actually learn of it till later. In 1943 after the Germans had moved further east and invaded the USSR, mass graves were uncovered in the Katyn forest, and identity documents showed that the bodies were those of the Polish officers captured by the Soviets in those first weeks of the war. Post mortem examination showed that the date of death must have been some time in early 1940. This murder of thousands of our Polish officers was to hang between the Soviets and the Poles for long years afterwards. In killing these men, the Soviets had slaughtered the best of our nation. These reserve officers were doctors, lawyers, academics, business and professional men, our natural leaders and the lifeblood of Poland. It was obviously necessary to slaughter them to take control of the country, for they were the ones who would have formed the challenge to Communist rule and provided the alternative. Such destruction was to be the policy of Nazis and Soviets alike with regard to Poland. My cousin Alexander was among the victims of Katyn.[4]

In Warsaw, as the last days of fighting dragged on in sleeplessness, fear and hunger, the population lived on rumours and on hope.

The word was spread, when capitulation was evidently drawing near, that the Prezydent of Warsaw was to address the city's inhabitants. He was a well-known figure and one whose name commanded universal respect in the city. He had organised much of the city's resistance to the invaders during these days of grim fighting, and had been responsible for keeping up our morale and our spirit. Everyone gathered around radio sets to listen to him. It was thus that we heard that the Polish forces had had to concede victory to the Germans.[5] The date was 28th September. We were all exhausted, many were wounded or ill, there were uncounted numbers of dead. We had virtually no food, water, or medical supplies. Basic facilities such as gas, electricity, or transport had long since ceased to function, and in parts of the city every other building seemed to be in ruins.

The battle which had raged with such ferocity was over. Against overwhelming odds an independent nation's army and air force, caught unawares and attempting in the final days to grapple with a fresh enemy in the east too, simply could not cope. Against the huge might of a National Socialist Germany which had been preparing for this conquest for many years, we were powerless without effective allies.

With capitulation, a city which had recently known the fury and horror of battle, came to know the equally sinister and awesome silence of defeat.

NOTES

Chapter 3

1. Poland's government had in fact left the city on September 3rd, heading for France, from where it would operate in exile.

2. Josef Garlinski writes in *Poland and the Second World War*: 'At 3 o'clock in the morning of 17th September, Molotov's deputy, Vladimir Potiemkin, summoned the Polish ambassador, Waclaw Grzybowski, and read him a note from his government. It dealt with the collapse of the Polish state, the disintegration of the Polish government and capital and the need to protect the life and property of the peoples of Western Ukraine and Western Byelorussia. Under the circumstances the Soviet government had ordered its forces to cross the Soviet-Polish frontier. The ambassador refused to accept the note and made a formal protest. By four o'clock that morning divisions of the Red Army were on Polish soil.' An agreement had been signed on 23rd August 1939 between von Ribbentrop, on behalf of Germany, and Molotov on behalf of the USSR, that 'in the event of a territorial and political transformation of the territories belonging to the Polish State, the spheres of interest of both Germany and the USSR shall be bounded by the line of the rivers Narew, Vistula and San'.

3. Bronislaw Mlynarski, writing in '79th Survivor' (Backman and Turner, 1976) described what happened to a friend of his who similarly owned an estate, Nowomalin, in the eastern part of Poland, and gives some insight into the common fate of such people: 'I learned from an eye-witness that when in the small hours of 17th September Soviet troops invaded Poland, Nowamalin was occupied in a matter of minutes and Karol's wife with all the guests (they had several refugees from Western Poland staying with them) and their children deported to an unknown destination. Karol himself was bundled as he stood into a car and taken to the nearest prison. that was the last thing that has ever been heard of him'.

4. The full details of the Katyn tragedy have been revealed in Louis Fitzgibbons' books 'Katyn: A Crime without Parallel' and 'The Katyn Cover-up'. These reveal the findings of the different commissions established to discover the facts about the murders. A memorial to the Katyn victims now stands in Gunnersbury, West London. For over forty years the Soviets refused to acknowledge the crime: finally in 1989, after the collapse of Communism in Europe, they admitted it.

5. The Prezydent was the equivalent of a Lord Mayor. Stefan
   Starzynski, 1893 – 1944, was nominated Warsaw's civil defence
   commissioner after the Polish government had had to leave
   the city on September 3rd. He set up a committee comprising
   representatives of the main political parties and worked closely
   with the military authorities to try to organise the defence of the
   city. After the capitulation he was briefly allowed to remain
   as Prezydent, but when the Nazis consolidated their rule over
   Poland he was arrested (27th October 1939) and imprisoned: he
   never returned.

Chapter Four

Warsaw was a city in ruins. The streets were filled with crushed barricades, dead bodies, rubble, and the detritus of battle. Many people were hungry, some were starving. It was a place of confusion with everyone hunting for members of their family. No one was left untouched. Over the next few weeks, some of our men started to come home to us. Edek, my brother-in-law, arrived at our flat. He had been fighting along Poland's western border, where the units had been forced back until they were eventually defending the outskirts of Warsaw. We were thrilled to see him, standing at our door in his battle-worn uniform. We rushed to hug him, and bombarded him with questions. The pleasure of the reunion was marred only by the discovery that he was only allowed to be with us for a few hours. He had to report back with the rest of his unit to be marched into captivity as a German prisoner-of-war.

Of course we all implored him not to go back. Why didn't he do what many others must be doing — take off his uniform, put on civilian clothes and go into hiding? He could slip into the countryside and eventually perhaps disappear over the border. But he was adamant that he had given his word of honour and must stick to it.

It's impossible to convey just how strong this sense of honour was among that generation of young Polish officers. It was something that really mattered to them — a code by which they were determined to live and a really vital and important force in their lives. This determination to keep his word took Edek back to the Germans, and into captivity.

Next came Janek, whom we had last seen departing from

the railway station back on September 3rd. He'd been badly wounded in the leg in the last days of the fighting around Warsaw and spent a few days in hospital, before making his way home. His wound meant that he had not been rounded up for imprisonment and felt under no obligation of any kind. He and Helena now discussed the future with urgency: he would remain hidden out of sight and later they might make their way to her parents' home, out in the country.

The victorious Germans marched into Warsaw: smart uniforms, shining boots, and − what I remember most of all − big round red faces. They did it all in great style, with a military band and much stamping about, while the grey-faced hungry people of the city looked on silently amongst the ruins left by the fighting.

On October 5th Hitler headed a victory parade through the city. Everyone living anywhere near his route was given special orders: we had to keep out of sight away from our windows under threat of savage punishment. It seemed absurd that the Germans were so terrified of us − but in a strange way it made us feel less powerless.[1]

For everyone, above the immediate worries over food and the whereabouts of missing members of families hovered the panic of the future: what were the Nazis going to do with Poland?

We soon found out. The country was divided into three zones. Over to the west the land was declared to be part of the Reich, and incorporated into Greater Germany. Poles were expelled from their homes and whole areas were given over to German settlers. This was part of the 'lebensraum', living-space, that Hitler had said his people needed. The central region of Poland − including Warsaw − was declared to be 'general government area', a sort of rump of our once-independent nation, and our eastern provinces had of course been given over to the Soviets.

There had been German-origin people living in Poland for generations. Many of them considered themselves to be in every way Polish citizens, with a commitment and loyalty to the Polish state. The loyalty of others was less certain. Under the new regime, all these people were invited to declare themselves as 'Volksdeutch', authentic members of the German race with all its trimmings of superiority over the rest of us. Some signed on the list because they genuinely felt German, others because they were threatened with death if they did not, others because of the extra rations and privileges that being Volksdeutch brought. Some went on living peaceably with their Polish neighbours, others became spies and informers, a permanent presence of the enemy among us. To their eternal credit, a few German Poles refused to go along with the Nazis by signing the Volkslist. Among these were many brave Protestant ministers, who opposed Nazism on Christian grounds — a number of these people perished in concentration camps or were executed.

These first days after capitulation were filled with rumour and counter-rumour. There were some suicides among young Polish officers who could see no other way out of the darkness that had engulfed our country. There were continued stories of spies and saboteurs who had deliberately impeded our war efforts and helped to bring about the German victory. There were fresh rumours about what the French and the British might do to help us: everyone remained certain that some plan was being hatched by the two great powers.

We heard that our government had escaped to France, and would work from that country for a restoration of our freedom. Polish soldiers, helped by their families and friends, were likewise slipping out, to make their way to join an army that was gathering in exile. Many were crossing the Carpathian mountains in Southern Poland, whilst others headed for Hungary or Rumania. Some were interned in the latter country in special camps, but sometimes the authorities turned a blind eye and allowed them to get away. When it became clear that capitulation was inevitable many of our soldiers were ordered to leave the country so that as many as possible should reach the Polish Army that was assembling together in France.

The makeshift military hospitals in Warsaw were filled with wounded Polish soldiers. They were kept under German guard. There was one about twenty minutes walk from Janek and Helena's flat: Szpital Ujazdowski, not far from Aleje Ujazdowskie. I and my friends went there as soon as we could after the capitulation, taking cigarettes, food, and news. There was a lot we could do to boost morale and give practical help to these officers and NCOs. I could write letters for those who were too badly wounded to write for themselves. Everyone was desperate for news of their families, and letters and notes begging for information or giving reassurance now began to criss-cross Warsaw. Just sitting and talking, offering a cigarette and a chance to find out what was happening in the city, was a help. More girls joined our group as we all spread the word to friends. I suppose in a way this was the beginning of my contact with the Polish underground movement because our presence in the hospital developed into an escape route for those struggling to join the Polish Army abroad. This was organised by one of my friends, a girl called Elzbieta.

We took the patients' Army greatcoats home, dyed them and altered them so that they would pass as civilian clothes, turning them from double-breasted to single-breasted and removing the epaulettes on the shoulders. Then we sneaked them back into the hospital. We also brought in genuine civilian clothes from our own families. The vital thing was speed — we had to get as many as possible of our officers out and into hiding in the city, from where they could go on to France.

The Germans started to put pressure on the hospital authorities to reveal the full names and ranks of all the patients. They wanted, of course, to get hold of the officers, NCOs and *podchorazych*, the cadet officers, because they saw them as potential leaders — the people who needed to be eliminated in order to crush any attempted uprising. They were not so bothered about ordinary soldiers. While the hospital staff stalled for as long as they could we worked feverishly to whisk away every possible man, using our wits and ingenuity.

We knew that at some stage the Germans would close the place down and evacuate all the patients to prison-camps back in Germany. Inevitably the day came when as I approached the hospital gates I was greeted by the sight we had all dreaded.

The hospital was a collection of buildings spread out over

wide grounds. As I hurried towards the entrance, the gates opened and some big army lorries, canvas-topped, roared through, all too evidently full of our men on their way to prison camps. A few managed to part the canvas at the back as the lorries went by and I saw their faces jostling for space to peer out. I was devastated. It was the end of our struggles, there was now no hope of rescuing them.

Warsaw was hungry. The Nazis were manifestly not worried about Polish people's welfare – it was being made increasingly clear to us that we belonged to a lower order of creation, fit only for slave labour. But the German Army, never as bad as the Nazi administrators who were shortly to follow them, did set up a soup-kitchen at one point. I watched some people going over to it and found hot tears welling up in my eyes. How could anyone bear to be humbled and crushed like that?

There was an eerie sort of pretence at normality about those first days after the capitulation, before things suddenly got more savage. Schools re-opened, and we went back to try to concentrate on forthcoming exams. We had this sense – all too well-founded – that this pseudo-normality was not going to last. Outright terror lay just below the surface.

There was a gradual development of life as it was to be lived under foreign occupation. The Germans erected loud-speakers in the streets blaring out official propaganda. We referred to it as dogs barking – a name that stuck. There was an official newspaper, too, which now appeared in Polish. Naturally it was only full of propaganda and all young Polish patriots boycotted it: we called it 'Gadzinówka' – the reptile paper.

We also agreed amongst ourselves to boycott the smart street cafés which the Germans patronised. Warsaw had always had a lot of these very attractive places where you bought a cup of coffee and sat and chatted while a singer crooned or a quartet played: foxtrots, tangos or the latest American music to which we had Polish words and which set our feet tapping. It was an extremely civilised way to spend the time, and now some of the cafés were gradually being re-opened as the rubble of the fighing was cleared. But most were now full of Germans and so

Poles — at least Poles of honesty and integrity — did not use them.

Then there was the problem of the cinema — all the newsreel films shown were full of scenes glorifying the German Army and telling us about its victories. So we all stopped going, and a saying went the rounds — 'Only pigs go to the cinema'. In Polish it makes a neat little rhyme, which we would repeat to one another.

At first, there was no public transport of any kind — there couldn't be, because all the tram tracks had been smashed up and twisted and buckled during the bitter street fighting. All travel around the ruined city was done on foot. We all plodded everywhere — to find relatives, to track down bits of food, to hunt for desperately-needed household goods, to get to school, to find out news. When bits of a tram service were re-started, the system operated completely differently from the way it had done in the old days. The front of every tram was now reserved 'Nür fur Deutsche' — Germans only. The old entry and exit system was abolished — formerly passengers had entered at the back and wandered up to get a seat and then left by the front. Now, the whole of the front section was for Germans, and we had to find odd spaces at the back and only use the back door.

The Germans put up big propaganda posters showing scenes of our ruined city bearing the caption 'Anglio — to twoje dzieło', 'England — this is your handiwork'. They were trying to convince us that all our suffering was Britain's fault — but no one believed that, of course.

Everyone's main priority was to locate lost members of their family. Gradually, news began to filter through about what was happening in the rest of Poland. The western provinces were to be incorporated into the German Reich. They had been the first to bear the brunt of the fighting. Fortunately, my sister Zofia and her husband and children had survived but they had lost their home and all their possessions. Before the fighting began, in the tense days of August, they had packed up everything they could from their beautiful home and sent it to Warsaw by goods train, but it never arrived. Bits of furniture, silver, and precious family heirlooms had vanished for ever.

We heard that Zofia and the children had reached Warsaw, but we didn't know if they had survived the last days of fighting when of course all normal communication was impossible. Mother and I now set out for their address and as we drew nearer we saw that it had been at the very heart of the battle. With each street it seemed that fewer and fewer houses had survived. We walked more slowly – we almost didn't want to reach the place, for fear of what we would see there. With hearts thumping, we moved slowly, not talking, not even daring to look at one another – and found that it was one of the few blocks standing and that the family was safe.

Jadwiga also arrived in Warsaw, leaving her baby daughter Maja, and Maja's nurse, back in the country. She had quite a story to tell: when fighting broke out in the area where they had been holidaying they were left stranded. Then, when it was over, Jadwiga's one thought was to head home to the city to find out if we were all right, and with no trains running she did it on foot, plodding along day after day, sleeping under hedges or in open fields.

Now at last we were reunited, and we were able to tell her that we had seen Edek and that he was safe, a prisoner of the Germans.

Jadwiga badly wanted to collect little Maja and also some household goods, and move into Warsaw. I volunteered to go back with her to collect anything useful – we also felt we might be able to get hold of some food while we were out in the country.

Everything was in chaos, with refugees crossing and criss-crossing the countryside. We dug up some potatoes from a field with our hands for food. Little Maja's nanny, who was a country girl, decided to go back to her own family. Jadwiga and Maja came to stay with us in Janek and Helena's flat, which began to feel very cramped.

Jadzia still hoped to be able to move into her own flat: she and Edek had in fact been planning to move to Bielany, a suburb further up the Vistula, as soon as possible. The flat was there waiting for them and she wanted to settle there when transport could be arranged.

We now knew about everyone in the family except Wanda,

who had been living over in the territory which was to be part of the Reich. Then we heard that Bronek, her husband, had been badly wounded in both legs and was in a German hospital. Wanda, who was pregnant, was all alone with little three-year-old Bolek. We held a family discussion and it was agreed that my mother would go to help her. She obtained the necessary permission and, partly because she spoke fluent German, was able to go and be with Wanda for the baby's birth.

But it was only some while later that we discovered the full terror of what went on in those Reich areas deemed by the Germans to be set aside for German settlement. One couple who suffered were later to become my parents-in-law, which is how I came to know their story. They lived in the town of Sieradz, where my father-in-law was a lawyer. He had had a stroke and was partially paralysed – this saved his life because when all the leading people of the town were arrested and marched out of their homes he was physically unable to go. The Nazi policy was to gather together all the teachers, doctors, legal officials and other potential community leaders and eliminate them in one swoop, and then disperse the rest of the population to remote rural areas. Being unable to walk he was not taken off to be shot and so he survived to be sent to a distant village. All Polish homes in Sieradz were occupied by German settlers.

The area now deemed to be part of the Reich included the whole of Western Poland from Pomeramia to Silesia, with big cities like Poznán, Lodz and Katowice. About ten million Polish people were living there in 1939.[2]

The weather was suddenly starting to get colder. We hadn't had a proper autumn. It had gone on being remorselessly sunny while we prayed for clouds and rain to block the German bombers over us – and now in a ruined city lacking shelter and heating and food we were to be faced with one of the bitterest winters Europe had known so far this century.

All Souls Day, November 2nd, is always observed with great solemnity in Poland. Families gather to light candles on graves of dead relatives and these are left burning all night. There were still no buses and trams on the route to the cemetery, so Mother, Jadzia and I walked there, to commemorate the dead, as we had done every year for as long as I could remember. This year there were so many new graves to visit, so many more deaths to mourn. The Warsaw cemetery on All Souls Day became what we always called 'a city of the dead', with every grave like a lit-up house and the little paths between them like streets in the glow.

On the way back we got a lift on a horse and cart — the nearest available thing to a taxi. We were lucky to get the ride, but were frozen through and went for a hot drink — ersatz coffee, the real thing having long since vanished from Warsaw — in a little coffee-hut. As we sat trying to thaw ourselves out, Jadzia's glove slipped from her lap onto the floor. A German officer nearby at once leapt up and returned it to her, clicking his heels and addressing her politely in French. We ignored him and were in no mood to favour him with any reply.

Of course, we did come to understand that some of the ordinary German officers and soldiers were different from the Gestapo and the SS, and that perhaps not all Germans were hard-line Nazis. I do remember an incident which dates from this period in Warsaw which shows one of them in this light. I had gone into a ruined church and whilst kneeling there I became aware of another visitor. Standing with his cap in his hands, at the back of the church, staring at the headless statues and the shattered remnants of stained glass in the bitter cold was a middle-aged grey-haired German soldier. I saw with surprise that there were tears running down his face.

Any sympathy I may have felt was however tempered by the sufferings of my own people. Another vivid memory is of a Polish soldier stripped of his belt and cap, stumbling and gasping as he was forced to run and keep pace with a German on a fast bicycle.

November marked a turning-point — suddenly a new and harsher regime was imposed on us. There was a round-up of prominent citizens — politicians, teachers, priests, writers, any potential leaders — and they were all taken off to prison. We knew they would be shot or sent to concentration camps.[3] There was speculation that all this was being done because our Polish National Independence Day, 11th November, was drawing near. This day marked the end of the First World

War. It had been honoured all my life by all Poles as the day which saw our emergence as an independent nation, after 180 years of division and rule by the Russian, Prussian and Austrian empires.

For pupils in schools the new clamp-down happened dramatically. The headmistress announced that the German authorities were closing down all secondary schools, universities and colleges. From now on the only institutions of learning allowed for Poles would be primary schools and places teaching crafts and trades. Spontaneously, the class wanted to make a gesture to express our common feelings of anger, frustration and bitterness. We had no intention of bowing down under this new oppressive rule, but from now on we would have to fight back secretly, fervently, and in the hope that all the savagery, executions and brutality that we had already witnessed would not crush us all. At the end of the day, we chose a poem to sum up our feelings. It was 'Tragic Freedom' by one of our country's greatest contemporary poets, Casimir Wiezynski. Our country's freedom had been lost just a few days short of its 21st birthday.

NOTES

Chapter 4

1. In fact, as Jan Nowak recalls in his book 'Courier from Warsaw', an attempt on Hitler's life was planned for this occasion by the embryo Polish underground army, but because of lack of precise information on the Führer's role in the parade, it was not carried out. At first it was not clear whether Hitler would in fact be taking part — when it was discovered that he was, it was too late to get the vital information across. The underground commander in charge of the operation could not get through to the man on the spot with the explosives, because all the surrounding streets were under heavy guard. Lacking the precise information necessary — an explosion which failed to kill Hitler himself and merely removed some German military figures would have been worse than useless, provoking savage reprisals for no real achievement — the order to fire was not given.

2. A terror operation code named *Unternehmen Tannenberg* was carried out in these territories just before formal annexation, and over 16,000 people were executed in a campaign aimed at stressing that these territories should not be occupied by Poles as they had been German before Polish independence in 1918. On 27th September one of the Gauleiters appointed to control the territory — Albert Forster who had been given the *gau* of Pomerania, said 'I was appointed by the Führer to represent German interests in this country, with the clear instruction to Germanicise the land again ... to eradicate within the next few years any manifestations of the Polish nationality of no matter what kind ... whoever belongs to the Polish nation must leave this country'. Polish families were usually only given a few minutes to collect their belongings before being deported. Source: Josef Garlinski 'Poland in the Second World War'.

3. It was in this round-up that Warsaw's Prezydent, Stefan Starzynski, was taken, 27th October 1939.

Chapter Five

The new crackdown settled the grim pattern for the future. However, if the Germans thought it would break our resolve they were wrong. Far from discouraging us it only served to stiffen our resistance.[1] On the very day that the headmistress announced the forced closure of the school, she also told us about arrangements that were being made to carry on our education in secret. We were asked to signal if we could offer space for classes to be held in our homes, and I was one of those who raised a hand.

So, very soon after the official closures our secret classes were active and thriving. I would be told that on such and such a day, at such and such an address, there would be lessons in maths, or history, or literature. We would all make our way to the appointed house singly, and at staggered times, so as not to attract any attention. Each day just one subject would be taught — and then homework would be allocated until the group could meet again.

We all had complete confidence in this system, and treated the lessons with great seriousness. Indeed, our studies seemed far more important now than they had ever done in peacetime. We recognised that the invaders were trying to wipe us out as a nation, and to destroy any vestige of our culture and heritage. It was up to us to preserve what we could and keep Polish learning alive until our country was again free to enjoy it openly.

Helena wasn't too happy about the flat being used for lessons and was convinced that we'd all be discovered and the whole family shot or rounded up for prison. Poor woman, she lived in a fear that was only to increase with Janek's membership of the secret undergound army and our whole family's commitment to fighting with the resistance.

Our secret lesson would usually take place with the pupils seated around one big table – a dining-room or kitchen table would be pressed into service. We would be a smallish group – of course you couldn't fit a whole class into someone's flat so we met in various teams. In the matriculation groups, in particular, the commitment to study was keen and earnest – we desperately wanted to pass our exams and not be cheated of this opportunity of having some sort of realistic future.

Every day brought new evidence of this crushing of all things Polish. The music of Poland's great composer, Chopin, was forbidden. You could be shot for listening to it or playing it. Not only the schools, but all the universities had been closed down. Many senior academics and top intellectuals were taken away to concentration camps. Many never returned.

We certainly knew about these camps. There was much talk about what was going to happen to Warsaw's large Jewish community, for the Nazi attitude towards Jews was extremely clear and growing week by week more menacing. We also knew about forced labour on German farms and in German factories. The Germans then started the terrifying raids – to drag in young men and women for these forced-labour schemes – which were to haunt our lives for the rest of the Occupation. It could happen anywhere – in the street, on a tram, in the cinema, or simply by knocking on doors of homes up and down an apartment block. A round-up, a *łapanka*, meant that people could be dragged away from their homes and families, never to be seen again. There was nothing as refined as notifying parents or being allowed to fetch a few belongings. Lorries would be standing ready, and people were pushed into them and hurtled away.

The new sudden clamp-down, following what had been a period of comparative calm just after the capitulation, brought a quality of horror to our lives that was to remain through all the following years. Making our way to secret school sessions we would see dead bodies in the street, grim evidence of another execution. I myself witnessed people being rounded up and shot. There is no way that you can adequately describe − or ever forget − such things.

At home, we adopted a certain attitude. We would defy all the invaders' rules, even if such defiance brought danger. When the order came to hand in all radios, we held a family discussion and agreed that, rather than hand our precious wireless set over to the Nazis, we would destroy it. We took it secretly and threw it in the Vistula.

Museums and libraries were closed, works of art removed, lists drawn up of books by distinguished Polish authors which were now officially banned. Sheer survival became a matter of determination and initiative. People had to think of new ways to support their families. For a while, Janek and Helena ran a small food stall at Zelazna Brama, selling whatever food had been brought in from the country.

The winter began in earnest, and as had been foreseen, it was a particularly hard one. Food was now very short indeed. What there was consisted of some very peculiar bits and pieces. Everything was what the Germans called *ersatz* − a substitute. We had ersatz coffee, made from goodness knows what substances and then bottled, ersatz jam, ersatz tea. There was no butter, and fats of all kinds were in extremely short supply. The bread was heavy and had a sinister sort of taste − mouldy and disagreeable. It caused bad stomach cramps if it was eaten when it was too fresh − it was better to let it stand for a day or two and dry out a little.

It was bitterly cold. Everyone's home was freezing − no one had any fuel. Many flats were also dark − gas and electricity had in many cases not yet been reconnected following the massive destruction of all such basic facilities in the bombing.

Christmas came and went but it was very different from the celebrations we had known in peace-time. There was no food to produce for the time-honoured Christmas Eve *Wigilia*, or vigil meal, with its thirteen different dishes (representing Christ and the twelve Apostles) made of fish and all the different fruits of the earth. And the essence of the meal − family togetherness − was hauntingly missing. Almost every family had someone missing or recently dead − in the fighting, in an execution or in one of the big deportations. From the east filtered through horrific reports of what was happening in the Soviet-dominated areas.[2] From the west came only endless confirmation of German consolidation of victory. The only thing that made it feel like Christmastime was that people filled the churches. I remember the atmosphere — the Christian message with its promise of hope and its emphasis on good ultimately conquering evil seemed to have an added poignancy.

Maticulation was still the next important stage of my life. The secret school authorities were not allowing the German occupation to deny Poland's students the right to acquire proper qualifications. Secret preparations were going ahead for our examinations. The Germans had closed down all the grammar schools, and my old school was now only allowed to be used for teaching younger children basic reading, writing and sums. But the school caretakers, who were two sisters and a brother, helped to arrange things so that our matriculation could take place. We were all brought in on several appointed days to do our written exams, while a careful watch was kept, and these three arranged to ring an internal electric alarm bell if there should be any signs of Germans in the street outside. We had all been told what to do: we were all sitting at separate desks, in the big hall, and had a teacher as invigilator, just as in pre-war days, and the atmosphere was exactly like that of any peace time examination. But we knew that stacked on the teacher's table were various handcrafts and in the school kitchen there was a cookery display — so that as soon as the alarm was sounded our examination papers could be whisked away and we could transform ourselves into a craft class. This was the only sort of class that was legal for Poles, as the Germans wanted to train us only for basic service jobs. But keeping our exams secret in this way was the teachers' worry and not ours as pupils — I just sat with my heart in my mouth hoping I'd be able to answer all the questions on the exam paper.

If we had been caught out, all of us, teachers and pupils alike, could have ended up in concentration camps. We were lucky: no German came near the school that day. The next stage was the oral exam and all this was arranged

in private houses. Our teachers risked everything to make
sure we got every chance to get fully accredited examination
opportunities.

The oral examination involved what was called a Com-
mission − you sat before three people to be questioned on
your chosen subjects. Organising this in complete secrecy
must have been no picnic for our teachers − but they did
it and I passed my matriculation knowing that I held fully
valid certificates in all subjects.

My dream of university was one that had to be abandoned now. There were secret university sessions − held in
private homes and hidden buildings, just like the secondary
schools − but the problem was one of money. Everyone
had to contribute what they could in order to finance the
professors and lecturers and enable them at least to eat
and survive. Having no money, I would have to leave the
fostering of Poland's culture and literature to others and
make alternative plans. In any case it was obvious that the
priority was to find work that would be of some practical
service to others.

I almost didn't have a future at all. Towards the end of
the winter, whilst Janek and Helena and I were out together,
a *łapanka* suddenly broke out in the street. We saw the German
soldiers and the lorries and we fled. The only hope was to
get into a nearby house. We rushed into an apartment block
and up to the top flor. There we hammered on the door and
begged for shelter. This was a dangerous thing to do. You
never knew whether or not a person was Volksdeutch, or
someone who might have some motive for denouncing you
to the Germans. But the lady opened the door and took us in
without asking any questions. Peeping from the balcony of
her flat, we saw the grisly scene beneath us: young men and
women being herded together and forced into a lorry which
then rolled away taking them to their fate. Our hearts were
thumping, because the soldiers might yet decide to instigate
a house search and check all the flats. But they had evidently
got their quota for the day. After a period of waiting, we
decided it was safe to go out again.

The early summer of 1940 was a black time for us. When
France fell to the Germans, it came as a terrible shock to

all Poles. There had been strong links between Poland and France for centuries. In the 19th century and the early part of this one, many well-to-do Polish families had tended to send their daughters to France or to employ French governesses as the girls grew to their teens. France had always been seen as central in European culture, ideas and civilisation. Like Poland, it was a Catholic country, sharing with us a traditional devotion to the faith which had shaped Europe's music, architecture and literature.

That France should fall had seemed almost unthinkable. Besides, our government was there — the one legal authority that Polish patriots recognised, and the central focus on which our schools network, exiled armed forces, growing underground movements and all other Polish activity centred. We learned that the Government had escaped to Britain and with it large numbers of our soldiers and airmen. Soon the latter would be fighting in the skies over Southern England, in what was to be called the Battle of Britain, the first of many foreign battle areas where Poles fighting under British command would give their lives.

Many Polish young men had joined the exiled armies, slipping away across our borders. Some went across the mountains, guided by the local mountain people who knew every nook and cranny of the area and were only too happy to help send another Polish fighting man to join Poland's potential liberators. Now the fall of France had forced our exiled government and soldiers to Britain, where they joined those of other occupied countries.

I had decided to take up nursing. It would be a worthwhile occupation, one in which I could be of some practical use — and it would offer me some security and somewhere to live. I decided to train with the Polish Red Cross. For the first three years of the German occupation, the Red Cross was allowed to continue with all the activities it had run before the war, including training nurses and running hospitals. Then everything was changed and according to international convention it was only allowed to run a missing-persons bureau.

The organisers of our Red Cross nursing school had merged it with another one — it became jointly the Warsaw

School of Nursing. This was to prove rather a clever move, because it ensured that those of us who had started our training with the Red Cross could complete our courses even after the Red Cross had been more or less closed down, and so get our diplomas and become qualified.

As a student nurse I lived in. This wasn't compulsory, but it suited me very well as I had no real home base of my own. Janek and Helena's flat, which was in a very attractive block, was suddenly commandeered by the Germans. It happened very quickly — they just turned up and announced that the area had been designated a Germans Only zone, and everyone had to get out and find themselves some accommodation elsewhere. No question of compensation or anything like that. As it happened, Janek and Helena were reasonly fortunate and found another flat on the other side of the Vistula — but the Germans would just as happily have turned them out into the street. Janek piled up their furniture and bits and pieces and they moved into their new home. It was a good thing they had somewhere to live as they now had a baby daughter, Eva. Jadzia was now living in Bielany further up the Vistula in the flat that she and Edek had chosen in those long-vanished days before the summer of 1939. Janek had helped her with the move, as it involved using a ferry to take her household goods up the river — this was cheaper than trying to go by road. Jadzia had to work to support little Maja and found a job with the Warsaw City Medical Department. She heard occasionally from Edek in his prisoner-of-war camp somewhere in the Reich. Another woman who had lost her home when her part of Western Poland was incorporated into Germany lived with her, looking after Maja during the day and helping with the cooking and cleaning.

At the nurses' home the accommodation was simple but comfortable. The rules of the place were strict and our lives were rather regimented; there were punishments, for instance, for such things as being unpunctual. But there was also fun and friendship. One of my room mates was a girl called Joanna, short and plump and with a good sense of humour. She used to tell disgusting medical jokes during meals and spoil our appetites — which suited her very well because she would then seize the opportunity of finishing our food. Together, we also shared the game of lining up the tinny aluminium spoons and then flicking one of them so that the whole lot rattled off the table together − and then assuming vague, innocent faces when our seniors from the top table came over to investigate. Pointless but enjoyable.

I soon discovered that for me the nurses' home was a great protection and a good cover for underground work, in which I now became deeply involved. My first links with it had come through Elzbieta, who had been the leader in our efforts to smuggle officers out of hospital to escape imprisonment. She had introduced me to the secret army and provided the first contacts. But now I made two more separate links with the underground movement. First, through Janek, I became attached to the 7th Polish Lancers regiment. This was not a complicated matter, as he was by now a member of this regiment, which had been given the code name of 'Jelen'. The regiment was part of what was to be known later as the Armia Krajowa, or AK − the Home Army of Poland.[3] When he heard I was in touch with the Underground through Elzbieta, Janek urged me to join his regiment: 'It's an old regiment, with a fine tradition behind it − and it would be good for us to be together.'

The main aim of the undergound was a full uprising in Poland. We didn't know the day or the hour: we were working and preparing and operating under orders from our Government. With the fall of France, all eyes were on London. We all accepted the government in exile there as the one true authority for Poland.

Janek's work was in training young men to fight. They needed to be taught everything, from basic drill to specific fighting tactics. It all had to be done under cover of secrecy, of course, and so we entered a world of code names, private signals and carefully memorised addresses. Janek chose 'Nalęcz', a part of our mother's family coat of arms, for his code name.

One day when I went to Janek and Helena's new flat, he waited until Helena was out of the room and then he said 'Look at this' and lifted up a couple of tiles in the parquet flooring. There in the space underneath, carefully wrapped in oiled rags, was a pistol. As he held it up, Helena came back into the room and let out a shriek. 'What are you doing? They'll come in − they'll find it − they'll kill us all!' Poor girl, it wasn't the same for her as for us − somehow we had got beyond the point of fear and were used to the idea of what was going on. For Janek, using the flat to hide part of the Home Army's slowly growing store of weaponry was simply part of his duties. But Helena's first thought was for the safety of her husband and their baby. Not everyone is cut out to be an underground soldier!

Around this time I also began to work for the underground in another capacity. This second involvement started rather curiously. During my first few months of training at the Warsaw School of Nursing, I saw quite a bit of an old school friend, Zoska. She was somewhat older than me and had been one of the senior pupils when I was in a lower form at school − I had always looked up to and admired her. She was a natural leader and had been prominent in the Girl Guides[4] − the sort of girl on whom younger ones were apt to have a 'crush'.

Zoska and her mother were very good to me during the early days of my life at the nurses' home. They must have guessed that the food there was very poor, because they often left me little packets of sandwiches made from whatever they had available, for which I was very grateful. They lived very near Janek and Helena's first flat, before the move across the Vistula.

I was always still a little bit in awe of Zoska − couldn't stop thinking of her automatically as the 'senior girl' who had to be treated with a degree of respect. One evening when I was round at her flat, I very badly wanted a cigarette. The war, the tension, the cold and the lack of food had set most of us smoking: we rolled our own from whatever tobacco or substitute was available. But smoking was one of the things that the code of the Guides had definitely ruled out. Once you had adopted this appalling habit, you had transgressed and fallen from grace. I didn't specially want Zoska to know I had capitulated. Eventually I couldn't bear it any longer. 'Zoska', I said diffidently, attempting what I hoped was a sophisticated shrug, 'I badly want a cigarette − do you mind if I smoke?' She grinned a bit sheepishly. 'Of course not . . . I smoke, too!' A barrier was broken and we were both chatting with a new intimacy as we lit up.

'What exactly are you learning on this nursing course — I mean, how confident do you feel about looking after badly sick people?' Zoska asked as we sat comfortably. I told her where we were up to — we were studying both theory and practice and, yes, already I was beginning to think and feel like a proper nurse.

'Do you know about the different bandaging techniques — about broken legs and things like that — enough to teach other people about it?' The conversation was getting more detailed — she wanted to know exactly what sorts of things we were learning, and whether I had a good grasp of the rudimentary techniques needed for various emergencies. Then it became clear what all this probing was all about — she had been asked by the underground to find someone to organise first-aid training for teams of girls all over Warsaw who would act as nurses and orderlies when the fighting began. I don't remember pondering for very long: it seemed automatic just to say 'Yes — OK, I'll do it'.

My work would involve going to homes where the groups were getting together, holding instruction sessions and organising examinations in the skills acquired. I was also to be part of the team gathering together vital equipment — bandages, cotton wool, antiseptics, splints — and hiding it around Warsaw.

Involvement with the Underground on two levels — with the Lancers and with the nursing units — brought a heightened level of danger. If I wasn't caught through one, I might well be through the other. I would have to be extra careful.

For my codename I chose my second name, Irena, and it was by that name that I was to be known to the people with whom I was to share the most memorable months and years of my life.

NOTES

Chapter 5

1. The new regulations were issued on 26th October, when Governor Hans Frank took command of the 'General Government' area of Poland. His proclamation to the Polish people informed them that they now lived under the protection of the German Reich and launched a campaign to eradicate every vestige of Polish identity.

2. In February 1940 the Soviets deported thousands of families from Poland's eastern provinces to distant regions of the USSR as slave labour. Travelling in locked trucks without food or water for several days many, especially small children, died on the journey. Larger numbers died in the camps where starvation rations, savage punishments, lice and dirt combined to take a high toll. For a moving account of this tragedy, see 'War Through Children's Eyes', edited by Irena Grudzińska – Gross and Jan Tomasz. Gros, Hoover Institution Press, California, USA, 1981, which gives surviving children's accounts, written after they were eventually brought out under the amnesty declared when war broke out between the USSR and Germany.

3. The AK grew out of the Union for Armed Struggle (ZWZ) which was later joined by various other groups. Plans for underground activity had been laid even while Warsaw was burning under the blitzkrieg in September 1939. The Union for Armed Struggle was formed in January 1940 and the name was changed to Home Army in February 1942 to emphasise its links with General Sikorski's government in London and the Polish Army fighting abroad. There were, of course, other underground groups, including Communist ones, but the Polish government in London repeatedly urged all groups to unite themselves under AK command.

4. During the Occupation, the Girl Guides went underground, and became the Szare Szeregi, the 'Grey Order', playing a very important part in the underground movement.

Chapter Six

My work for the Resistance introduced me to aspects of life I could not have envisaged a few months before. Working for the Underground I developed a procedure to minimise risk. I would stand outside an apartment block, scanning the names by the main door to see which bell I should ring. Finding the name, I would press the bell, trying to think quickly about something else, to obliterate the name from my mind. I carried around with me one haunting fear which was to be ever-present when I was engaged on underground work — the fear of torture and of giving away information if I was captured. We were all under no illusions — we knew perfectly well that the Gestapo headquarters in the Aleja Szucha had plenty of modern equipment to use on anyone suspected of harbouring information about the Resistance.[1]

Looking back, I can honestly say that I was not really afraid of dying. Death was all around us, all the time. People disappeared from their homes or were shot in reprisal-killings by the Nazis after some infringement of their rules and regulations. My one fear was that under pressure of torture, acutely and knowledgeably applied, I would collapse and tell them what I knew. Throughout this period this was to be my abiding fear.

We had been told, of course, that if we were captured we must consume or destroy any message that we happened to be carrying. Undoubtedly the greatest protection lay in knowing as little as possible — about the person to whom you were delivering the message, the person who sent you, and the wider picture of what it all meant. You just got on with the task and didn't ask unnecessary questions.

'I'm Irena.' When the girl answered the door we said the minimum necessary to identify ourselves. Upstairs in the flat the team of trainee first-aiders rose when we entered. The atmosphere was formal and military: they lined up and their leader gave the official report to me — how many members in the group, how many present and how many absent. Then we got down to work. As I look back I remember their faces, solemn and dedicated as I ran through the information I wanted to get across to them that evening. We had the minimum of equipment but they took turns at practising the various bandaging skills and repeating after me the different treatments. They all knew they had to reach a certain standard. The underground army had its own examining system and everyone aimed at becoming qualified first-aiders (Sanitariuszki). Once the training session had finished, we would all leave separately at intervals. It would have looked suspicious had it become known that a lot of young people were gathered together at one house.

These training sessions were only one part of my underground work. I was also now a liaison girl with the underground army — a job that involved passing on written orders and messages. Girls were the best choice for this work as we seemed to excite less suspicion than young men as we went about the city. I quickly discovered that not only did the nurses' boarding school provide a safe and secure base from which to operate, but going about in nurse's uniform was a great protection. It was about the only thing that the Germans seemed to respect. They appeared to have a horror of epidemics breaking out. We soon realised, for instance, that you stood a chance of keeping them out of a building if you hinted that there was an infectious disease inside. They seemed to think, in any case, that we were all dirty peasants riddled with revolting illnesses and living in squalor. We were happy to let them think like that if it afforded us a bit of cover for the work of liberating our country.

Out on any underground activity, I would dress in my uniform and carry my little box of nursing kit with a syringe. If challenged, I could say that I was on my way to give an emergency injection.

Great though the deprivations were for all the citizens of the city, it now became clear that the greatest tragedy centred on Warsaw's Jewish community. In 1940 the Germans began herding them together in one area — the section of the city that was later to become the Warsaw Ghetto. It was an old part of the city where the narrow streets ran close together and had curious names which echoed a medieval past. It had always been a traditionally Jewish area, but now many more were sent to live there, turned out of their own homes in the suburbs or in the big apartment blocks.

It became a serious crime — a capital offence — to hide a Jew.[2] It was only much, much later — after the end of the war — that I discovered that Jadwiga sheltered a Jewish lady and her child in the basement of her home in Bielany for almost two years. Jadwiga was also involved in other extremely risky work, trying to smuggle messages in and out of the Paviak prison. This involved finding some warder who could be bribed or made to co-operate and using him to send in tiny messages in what were called 'grips' — fragments of thin paper on which vital news and information could be crammed in the smallest lettering possible.

We all felt helpless at the plight of the Jews. People could help individuals here and there, but it was impossible to organise anything on a massive scale as we simply didn't have the resources. The Ghetto became an established fact. The Germans built a wall around it and a main road ran alongside on which trams travelled. These went very fast on the stretch past the ghetto without stopping.

My life was now very full: my official training as a student nurse was very demanding, with academic work to do as well as the practical nursing side, and then in every spare moment I was working with the underground.

One night one of the doctors under whom I was training was killed in the Ghetto. He had gone there following an emergency call — he was one of the very few people who had been allocated a special pass which allowed him to go behind the wall. He never came back and none of us ever discovered exactly what had gone on, except that we knew he had been shot by the Germans. Even extending the most ordinary humanitarian services to Jewish people involved the risk of death.

I am sure that by this stage my mother knew that all her children were involved with underground work to some degree, but when we met up we naturally never discussed what we were doing. Whether it was as a liaison girl, a team leader or simply someone whose home was being used for a meeting, the rule of silence prevailed.

My fear of retaining information which I might release under torture gave me a habit of instantly forgetting names and addresses which became lifelong. I would deliberately erase from my mind the surname after I had found it on the list of apartments in the main entrance hall, and I taught myself to see all the young girls I trained simply as blank people without proper identification. It was curiously effective. Even now I cannot remember names and addresses very well, even when I want to remember them.

For meetings of the secret army teams, or the passing on of orders, we operated a communication chain. 'A' would tell 'B' who would tell 'C' and so on. You never wanted to know more than you needed – you just passed the message to the next person down the chain and that was your duty done. This chain worked pretty efficiently operating on this principle, which avoided overlap and confusion as well as ensuring secrecy. Its obvious drawback was that the chain could be broken if one person was away from home. Much later, when the Rising finally started, some people failed to make their appointed posts because of this.

Meanwhile the shortages of food started to become extremely serious. The food by now in Warsaw was terrible. Butter was unavailable except on the black market. Margarine was issued in tiny chunks. There were jams made from the most amazing things. There was very little meat. People would have died of hunger if it had not been for the peasant people from the countryside around the city who brought food into the town.

The penalty for selling food on the black market was death. The country folk were not allowed to bring their meat into the city as they had traditionally done. Everything was subject instead to quota and ration systems. There were some amazing incidents in connection with this. Of course, the farmers used to smuggle meat in somehow. We heard different tales about how this was done.

On one occasion some people managed to bring in a pig disguised as a woman. They made use of the German fear of sick people. Having killed the pig, they stood it up on its hind legs and dressed it up in an old skirt and coat. (It was winter, so the pig was frozen hard). They wrapped a thick headscarf round to obscure its head and face and propped it up between two people on the train, who chatted to it soothingly, making it very clear to anyone passing that this was a very sick old woman brought into the city for urgent medical treatment. No German wanted to go too near to ask questions. It was dodges like this that provided food for hungry city-dwellers during the Occupation.

Around this time I took my formal oath of allegiance to the Home Army. This was something of an honour as you weren't invited to do this until they were absolutely sure of you. I received a summons − through the now highly developed Home Army secret communication chain − to be at a certain flat at a certain time, and when I arrived I found I was one of several young people taking the oath prior to an AK meeting. It was just an ordinary sitting-room, of course, and we waited without talking to one another, wondering what was going to happen.

Presiding over the ceremony was a regular officer of the Polish Army, one who had been properly commissioned before the War. On a table beside him stood a crucifix, with candles burning on either side of it: one by one we went forward, to place our hands on the Cross and make the solemn promise that bound us to fight for the liberation of Poland, to obey the orders of our superiors, to maintain absolute secrecy whatever the cost. The use of the Cross meant that this oath was a pledge given under the name and seal of Jesus Christ, and there were no false theatricals about what we were doing. 'Put the first two fingers of your right hand on the base of the Cross, like this,' I was told, and by the flickering light of the candles I made the promise with a deep-rooted understanding that the words summed up the very core of all that we were doing.[3]

Cut off as we were in our own little world, we nevertheless heard a surprising amount of news as it was passed around by word of mouth. Some members of the Underground were also specifically responsible for listening to the radio, and others for communicating back to London. Then we had our underground newspapers, passed from one trusted person to another. Thus, in 1941 we heard that Germany had attacked Soviet Russia. We were not completely surprised. When the news was confirmed as true, our initial reaction was that at least this showed that Poland's two historic enemies were now at each other's throats.

The war entered a new stage. We saw the massive German troop movements as their army swept eastwards, pouring through Warsaw and across the Polish countryside. The German radio programmes started to boast about the great victories on Soviet soil.

We had no love for the Soviets, but they were a massive and powerful force which we felt would eventually help to break the back of Nazi Germany. The London radio urged us on to optimism. We continued our preparations for an eventual uprising with dedication and enthusiasm.

The Nazis showed no sign of slackening their grip on Poland or worrying about the future. They still spent a great deal of time and energy in attempting to eradicate all signs of Polish life and culture.

In the centre of Warsaw there had stood for years a statue commemorating the great astronomer Copernicus, who had been born in Poland. The Germans now removed the original plaque and replaced it with another one which appeared to make the claim that he was of German origin. The statue became a rallying-point for people who wanted to affirm their Polish identity or make fun of the Germans. Three or four young men, friends of mine, decided to meet there on one particular anniversary connected with Copernicus and lay red and white flowers, representing our national colours, at the statue's base. Since all gatherings of any sort were banned, this was a risky and even a foolhardy undertaking. When they saw what was happening, the Germans opened fire. Most of the group managed to escape but one of them, the fiancé of Halszka, a close friend of mine, who was a student nurse alongside me, was hit and badly wounded. He was brought to the hospital where I was working.

When he was examined, we all knew that he had not long to live, because he had been hit in the liver and the blood was pouring out. It was a terrible wound. The flow of blood was unstoppable and obviously fatal. We did what we could. I got permission from the nurses' training school to go and help look after him. Halszka had already been sent for. He was lying white-faced on the bed, all too obviously close to death. They were able to talk together, and they decided to get married then and there — their vows their final gift to one another.

A priest came. I was one of the small group that gathered by the bed, and heard the frail boy's voice and the young girl's stronger one quietly repeating the words of the beautiful wedding promises which everyone normally associates with life and hope and happiness. I was one of the formal witnesses to the ceremony. None of us could look at one another. The young couple remained side by side until he died.

If death seemed a big price to pay for a patriotic gesture, it needed to be seen against the wider scene of what was taking place all over our country. We knew about dreadful camps into which people were being herded, starved and beaten to death. We knew about what was happening to Jews. They were being ruthlessly hounded by the German authorities. Many of the top people in the major professions in Warsaw, notably medicine, were Jewish and now they were all being forced into the barricaded ghetto to await deportation to — where?

Our efforts to hide and help them seemed pitiful in the face of their plight ... and worse was to come, when the ghetto was finally destroyed and mass murder commenced in earnest.

We knew there was a big concentration camp at Oswięciem (Auschwitz) not far from Krakow. It seemed to be a complex of different sectors. Most people who went there never returned; others in different parts of the camp, did survive to be sent elsewhere and a few were even released when their terms of arbitrary imprisonment were over. One patient who arrived at the hospital at this time had spent some time there. He was Krzysztof Kamil Baczyński, a brilliant young man who was already making a name for himself as a poet. He and I became friendly and he dedicated some poems to me. The feeling among all Polish young people of our generation in Warsaw was passionately patriotic. The oath of secrecy to the AK stopped any talk or even hints about anti-German activities, but a common loyalty to the cause was deep-rooted among us. Krzysztof was in fact, like me, in the underground army though I did not learn this until we all came out into the open in the 1944 Rising. But our mutual commitment was simply something taken for granted. It was one of the things that helped to make all wartime boy/girl relationships so intense. Krzysztof and I did become close — but I wasn't ready for anything serious yet and I knew it. Much later, I heard that he married someone else.

My training period as a nurse finally came to an end and I took and passed my qualifying examinations. Despite wartime conditions, we held a traditional-style ceremony at which diplomas were handed out by the Principal of the training school. Family and friends gathered for the celebration and we posed for photographs. Standing there with posies of flowers, wearing our uniforms freshly washed and looking the best we could, new graduates of the Warsaw School of Nursing, was satisfying. Black velvet bands across our starched caps proclaimed our diploma status. I felt I had finally reached adulthood and now the future stretched ahead of me. Perhaps this feeling was naive as we were all hemmed in by the German Occupation and the grim reality of war.

Under the terms of my nursing training I had made a commitment to work at 'Dom Bodouena', a home for orphaned or abandoned babies. So I started the job as a nursing tutor. It was at Nowogrodzka Street, just out of the city centre, and was run by the Sisters of Charity. These nuns were well known in almost every European country. They wore a distinctive, vast form of headdress which was recognisable everywhere and they ran a huge network of institutions of one kind or another across the continent.

The war was rapidly approaching one of its blackest

moments. The situation was getting more and more grim. Underground work provided the only outlet for pent-up anxiety and outrage, and our only hope for the future. When the Jewish Ghetto was burned in April 1943, a feeling of anguish and horror swept the city. Hundreds of people in the Ghetto were either killed outright, deported to camps or hunted down gradually in the bitter drawn-out horror of its last days. We had so few guns or ammunition and the enemy was so overwhelmingly powerful. Some help was given to the Jewish resistance − but the Home Army simply didn't have the resources to do more. Being unable to give adequate help was the worst horror of all.

The one cause for hope was the unity of ordinary people in their opposition to the Nazis. There was never any question of the Germans forming a puppet government from amongst Poles. Opposition was passionate and vital. It included the whole range of activities normal to the life of a nation. Traitors were tried by Polish courts, schoolchildren educated, students awarded degrees − all in an underground network that owed its allegiance to our government in London. There was also a cultural life − people gathered in tiny groups for Polish music and poetry readings, keeping alive our arts and fulfilling our needs.

There was one ward in the Nowogradzka children's home which was set aside specifically for training purposes, and this was under my charge. When I arrived, the home included many Jewish children and young Jewish mothers and babies who had escaped from the Ghetto. They were hiding here under the shield of the nuns, who were risking their lives to give them the protection they needed. The home had always had a tradition of privacy and discretion, because in the past it had offered a refuge for young unmarried mothers: people regarded it as a place where people had a right to retain their own dignity and not to be open to outsiders. Everyone knew the penalty for hiding Jews − it was death, as simple as that. One way to keep fear at bay was never to refer to what was going on. We treated the Jewish mothers and babies as we treated anyone else, and simply didn't refer to what was obvious to all. The nuns managed to keep up the tradition of the place even in the middle of a war and a foreign occupation – they tried to maintain a sense of privacy about the home and a remoteness from the authorities.

The home consisted of different buildings set in an enclosed park. We had our own rooms in one building, and the different wards were spread about the grounds. One morning, very suddenly, at about 4 am, we got word that the whole place was surrounded by the Gestapo.

Every one of us had something to hide. We were all – including the nuns and the chaplain – absolutely up to our necks in underground work of various kinds. None of us had ever spoken about it to one another, but it was there as an undercurrent all the time, and now it bubbled to the surface. The one thought uppermost in every mind was of papers that needed hiding or destroying. Bleary-eyed and half-dressed, we were nevertheless all running about hurrying things away, stuffing them into secret places, cramming them into odd corners. It was actually almost comic the way we all scurried about as realisation dawned of the grim predicament we were all in – and still none of us said a word about what we were all doing!

We were extremely fortunate in the Sister Superior, Sister Stanislaus – Sister Starsza, as we called her. She was a very intelligent woman and she started to keep the Germans talking. On and on she went, answering their questions in the most long-winded way she could, talking and persuading for more than two hours. She kept insisting that there was absolutely nothing for them to see except some little orphan children and unmarried mothers being looked after by nuns and nurses.

All the rest of us, one by one, gathered in the chapel. The grey light of dawn was filtering through the windows. The priest knew all about our underground work – he was a chaplain in the Home Army – but even as we gathered to pray, none of us mentioned a thing. We just knelt there and with nerve-wracking intensity tried to put our petitions up to God. The atmosphere was taut. We had no idea what was going on and whether Sister Starsza would be able to outwit these men or not.

I will never know what happened. All I can say is that after two or three hours the Gestapo left. Sister Starsza had kept them talking and eventually they went away without discovering a thing. Was it God's protection? Certainly the home had been placed with total faith in His hands. In any case, none of us ever found out exactly what had happened. It came into the category of things that you simply never talked about.

Later that day when I went into the children's ward I threw up my hands with a sudden fresh recognition of just how appalling it would have been if the Gestapo had managed to set foot inside. One glance at these mothers and children, with their dark curly hair and sensitively-shaped faces, would have told them that they were Jewish. Physically, Polish Jews were very distinctive, with facial shapes quite different from the broad Slavonic one. There wasn't any room for doubt, and one glimpse inside that ward would have sealed everyone's fate.

The lowest time for every Pole was the summer of 1943 when General Sikorski, the leader of our government in exile in London, was killed in an air crash. He had represented our link with our western allies, our hope for freedom. There was a little verse we all said about him — 'Sloneczko wyżej, Sikorski bliżej', 'The sun higher — Sikorski nearer'. To us, he represented the springtime, and all our hopes. We really were convinced that the British and the French were doing their best to come to our aid, and Sikorski's death destroyed the strongest personal bond we had with them.

A new leader was chosen by our government but nothing would ever be quite the same. A certain optimism had somehow vanished that would never return. It was replaced by grim determination.

It was about the time of Sikorski's death that we first heard of the discovery of the bodies of hundreds of our Polish officers, missing since 1940. They had been prisoners of the Soviet army following the latter's invasion of the eastern part of our country back in September 1939. The Germans, pushing eastward, had uncovered a series of mass graves in Katyn forest: it became evident that these bodies were those of our officers, slaughtered by the Soviets some time in early 1940.

At first we thought that this news, coming as it did from

the Germans, must be simply yet another propaganda trick. But it became clear that on this occasion they were stating the truth: all the facts fitted. We heard that our government in London was demanding a full enquiry under the International Red Cross, and that the Soviets were refusing to co-operate. It gave us no satisfaction to contemplate that it was this same Soviet army which was officially allied with Britain and France, the countries on which our hopes for liberation were focused.

NOTES

Chapter 6

1. It included dental equipment. Years later I was to meet a priest who told me exactly what it was they did to him. I have never been able to forget it, although I wish I could.
2. The following proclamation from the SS and Police Chief in Warsaw, dated 6th September 1942, is quoted by Janina Bauman in *Winter in the Morning*, her account of her life in the Warsaw Ghetto and beyond (Virago 1986). She gives her source of information as Josef Banas, *The Scapegoats*, translated by Tadeusz Szafar, Weidenfeld and Nicholson 1979:
   PROCLAMATION:
   Re: Death Penalty for assistance to Jews who have left Jewish residential areas without permission.

   Numerous Jews have recently left the Jewish residential areas to which they were assigned without permission. They are still for the time being in the Warsaw district.

   I hereby declare that by the third decree of the Governor-General concerning residential restrictions in the Government-General of Oct.15.1941 (UBL Gs p.595) not only will Jews who have in this way left the residential areas assigned to them be punished with death but that the same punishment will also be imposed on any person who knowingly harbours such Jews. This does not only include shelter and food but also any other sort of assistance, e.g. by conveying Jews in any sort of vehicles, by purchase of Jewish goods, etc.

   I hereby instruct the population of the Warsaw District to

inform the nearest police station or police command post immediately of any Jew who stays without authorisation outside a Jewish residential area ...

Warsaw,   The SS AND POLICE CHIEF
6 September 1942   Warsaw District

3. The original form of oath, devised with the help of a priest for the Union for Armed Struggle, was as follows: 'Before God the Almighty, before the Virgin Mary, Queen of the Crown of Poland, I put my hand on this Holy Cross, the symbol of martyrdom and salvation, and I swear that I will defend the honour of Poland with all my might, that I will fight with arms in hand to liberate her from slavery, notwithstanding the sacrifice of my own life, that I will be absolutely obedient to my superiors, that I will keep the secret whatever the cost may be.'

Chapter Seven

There were a number of Jewish girls among the student nurses. One was a girl called Hanka, who had escaped from the ghetto with her father, who was a doctor. We became friendly.

Running the children's ward with me and sharing the work of supervising the young trainee nurses was my colleague Sophie. She was much older than me — in her early 40s — and was plump and efficient. She came originally from Poznan, in the part of Poland now deemed to be officially within the Reich, and had fled to Warsaw to be in the marginally less harsh 'general government' district.

As a tutor and nursing sister I enjoyed my job and felt confident with my qualifications. My underground work was also becoming demanding. I was now attached to the small unit with which I would actually serve on the day of the open uprising against the Germans. The team leader was a young medical student, Wlodek, who had almost completed his training for becoming a doctor. We got on very well together: there was a great sense of comradeship at all underground meetings between all the young people involved.

Wlodek and I together arranged what we would need for the day when the fighting began. He had access to funds — I don't know how — and I made out lists of items and he acquired them. It was basic first-aid stuff: bandages and antiseptics, ointments and painkillers, splints and disinfectants. I never knew how he got everything, but he acquired it all somehow, and it all had to be hidden away until the day when it would be finally needed.

One day Wlodek told me that I had to go for an official AK examination to test my nursing knowledge. It struck me as a bit unnecessary since I was already a fully qualified nurse. But this is the way military things work, and I duly noted the date and address at which I was to report. It was, of course, only an ordinary home address and the whole thing had to be kept completely secret. On the tram I spotted Olga, who had been my tutor when I had been a student nurse. She was in the AK too! We both passed — the questions were very basic and straightforward. I was not to see Olga again until we met in the very different circumstances of a city which had finally erupted into open fighting.

Most of my friends were active in some way in the Underground — but we never spoke of it. Our views and feelings were well known to one another, but the nature of our active commitment was something we each kept strictly secret: we were all under oath. When we got together, as a crowd of young people, there was a sense of solidarity and common values that didn't need, in any case, to be spelled out in any detail. We were all Polish patriots. We allowed our feelings to show in our songs: we sang about our country, its history, and our longing for freedom, gathered around a piano in some one's flat, in music that became part of the very heartbeat of our lives. You had to be careful about being overheard: singing patriotic songs could mean a trip to the Gestapo, and death. Evening gatherings had other problems, too: the curfew meant that it was impossible to go out and about at night. Anyone found on the streets after the 'police hour' could be shot or hauled in for questioning and in all probability end up in a concentration camp. Getting together with friends thus often meant sleeping on someone's sofa or floor for the rest of the night.

The bonds of friendship were very special and very strong — we knew that we depended on one another, and there was a warm, understood feeling of loyalty and trust that was a bright thread binding us together. Sometimes the older people didn't understand about how we felt: there was criticism of the way we met to sing and have fun together. They really didn't know the way life was for us: the strain of maintaining secrecy, of holding information that could bring capture and torture, and the fever of wanting events to move more quickly and of having to bide time, and await orders. And we were all ordinary young people who in a normal way would have wanted to dance or go to shows and have fun. Instead, we simply enjoyed ourselves in the only ways available to us in our occupied city. We weren't being flippant when we met over ersatz coffee in a cold flat with some one humming one of our special songs that gradually everyone took up ...

Krystyna Krachelska was a popular singer at our gatherings. She wrote beautiful poetry, and songs which she sang herself. She was a pretty girl, and back before the war had been used as a model for the siren lady statue which was the official symbol of Warsaw, on the shore of the Vistula. Another member of our special crowd was Zbyszek: he was a schoolfriend of Janek's and now serving with him in *Jelen*.

During a working day we were all treated like people who had no basic rights in their own city: restrictions imposed by the occupying Germans reached every area of common life and were backed by savage punishments. But when we gathered together we could create our own pool of Polish freedom around us, and look to the day when we could claim our own country back again.

Some of the best and most memorable songs were written by two brothers, Jan and Andrew Markowski, both of whom had growing reputations as poets and songwriters. The songs had a down-to-earth poignancy because they were about things we really experienced. Andrew wrote moving, idealistic poetry and Jan, who was older, stirring songs with echoes of Poland's military past throbbing in them.

We sang some of Krzysztof Kamil-Baczynski's songs, too. There was a sense in which the poetry of this generation had a special mood of unity with the poetry of Poland's past. We all knew our history: our country had been divided by invaders before, and the freedom to affirm a Polish language and culture had been hard-won. We wanted to be worthy of the sacrifices of the past, and not fail in our own duty of fighting for our people's rights in this latest war.

Things were now beginning to take a new shape as far as

our country's future was concerned. The tide had begun to
turn for Germany, and the Soviet Army was beginning to
push forward from the east, regaining lost territory and
rolling forward every day and week towards us.

Few Poles trusted the Soviets. Russia was our ancient
enemy. For over a hundred years she had ruled large
stretches of our country, and the rule there had been harsh.
We disliked and feared this vast country which threatened
us from the east, and we disliked even more its savage
Communist system of government, and its atheistic base.
For a long while rumours and terrible bits of news had been
reaching us in Warsaw about what had been taking place in
the Polish villages and towns occupied by the Soviets in 1939.
We heard of men shot, women and children crammed into
cattle trucks and taken miles away to the further provinces
of the Soviet Union in conditions of starvation, thirst, and
filth, dead babies and elderly folk tossed out to lie unburied
on the way. We heard about open killings and deportations
designed to terrify those who had managed to remain behind
into submission. Some people had managed to escape across
to us in German-occupied territory with appalling news of
what had happened to members of their families and to
neighbours and friends.

We were all acutely aware that if the Soviets seized the
opportunity of grabbing the whole of our land as they rolled
across it in pursuit of the Germans, we would not get it back
again. The radio news from London − passed around in
secret − conveyed to us the urgency of our situation and
reminded us that we still had a legitimate government and
friendly allies.

The plan, as it emerged to us in the AK as 1944 opened,
was that each Polish city would be liberated by its own Polish
home forces before the Soviets could claim it as theirs. The
vital thing was going to be the timing. The AK must be ready
to strike when the critical moment came. As the Germans
retreated, we must harry and hound them out, seizing the
city and establishing a legal administration which would be
there to greet the Soviets and establish suitable necessary
relationships with them.

We felt that the Western allies would not allow a *fait*

accompli by the Soviet forces and would, on recognising our right to our own cities, give us all the backing they could once we had provided all the initiative in tackling what needed to be done in the first stages. We would have to fight hard and hold on firmly. The one impossible idea — the thing that we all rejected — was simply doing nothing and allowing ourselves, once the Germans had gone, to be trampled over by a neighbouring army which would establish itself on the ground and prove virtually impossible to dislodge.

Our plans and manoeuvres thus now took on a more specific shape and direction.

By the summer of 1944, everyone could feel things boiling up towards a climax. The Germans were retreating across Poland, harried by the advancing Soviet army. In July came the news of an attempted assassination of Hitler by officers of the German army. It had failed — but it seemed to be part of the general picture of a Nazi tyranny on the brink of a downfall.

Among young people in Warsaw, the longing to get on with the action, to be rid of the years of waiting, was now acute. More and more as AK members we felt that our hour was coming, that we would soon be able to take our place alongside our fighting allies and do our own part by winning back our own city and country.

The mood of the Germans in Warsaw was changing. There was uncertainty in the air. You could see some of them — then it became a lot of them — preparing to move out. In the last days of July the exodus became so noticeable that everyone was commenting on it. Troops seemed to be marching about a lot — there were gatherings of lorries and equipment. German civilians seemed all to be taking off westwards.

But there was still fight left in them — they were not giving up without a struggle. A new proclamation was suddenly made, calling up all remaining able-bodied Polish men for special labour in the Reich. Rumours swept the city about this — it was said that a date had been set and that plans were going ahead for tearing people forcibly out of their homes and workplaces. And the Polish reaction — both from those within the AK and ordinary civilians — was emphatic.

'They won't take us without a fight'. If necessary, with or without orders, we would simply oppose the Germans with all the force we had.

Looking back, I must make it clear that if General Bor — leader of the AK in Warsaw — and our Government back in London had not authorised the Rising, I think some of us would have done something anyway. For five long years we had watched our friends and neighbours being killed, and our country enslaved. We had been told again and again by our allies that Poland was the focal point of the war. We could not wait to be fought over again by others at this crucial stage: we had to turn the Nazis out ourselves, and assert our claim to our own territory.

It was in this atmosphere that I got my orders to attend what turned out to be my last AK briefing. The usual communication chain operated, and I was setting out to go to the agreed address when my mother suddenly turned up. She had just been popping in to visit me. 'Oh, Mamusia ... I'm just on my way out to a meeting — I'm in a hurry —' We chatted very quickly and briefly but I didn't pause to stay any length of time with her. Expecting to be able to return her visit any time within the next couple of days, I hurried off. She said she understood — of course I hadn't told her it was an AK meeting I was attending, but she was used to secrecy and to asking few questions. We made a brisk goodbye. She looked somehow so small, rather sad and vulnerable, going down that Warsaw street while I rushed off in my enthusiasm.

That was the last I was ever to see of her.

At the meeting, we were all given our final orders. Wlodek was there. Our assigned position was a chemist's shop in Pulawska Street. I would be heading a nursing team, with a couple of the girls from among those I had been training in groups all over Warsaw.

As the gathering ended, we wished each other good luck, and shook each other's hands. From now on it was just a case of waiting for the final hour.

Chapter Eight

'Soldiers of Warsaw!
Today I have issued the order you have been waiting for,
the order to begin open battle against Poland's age-old
enemy the German invader. After nearly five years of
uninterrupted and heavy fighting underground, today you
will carry your arms in the open in order to free your
country again and render exemplary punishment to the
German criminals for the terror and crimes committed on
Polish soil.
Warsaw, 1 August 1944
Chief Commander of the AK
Bor.'

I was at work when I got the order about the Rising. It was
Friday, July 29th, during the afternoon. Because I was at
the end of our particular communication chain, I didn't have
to pass the word on to anyone else — I just had to pack
up and go. The order at this stage was to stand ready: we
would be given the exact command to commence operations
a little later.[1]

This was it — the climax of all the years of waiting.

Rather prosaically, this momentous news caused awk-
wardness at work. By now I was conditioned to be secretive
about anything connected with the underground, and I
couldn't therefore explain why I intended to drop everything
I was doing and scurry off immediately. After all, no one in
their right mind would suddenly announce 'I'm a member
of the underground army. We're going to have an uprising.
Please may I go and join in?' Instead I had to make do

with odd taut phrases: 'I've had some news. I've got to be away for a while. I don't know how long it will be for ... I'm terribly sorry.' Sophia was cross. She looked at her watch and said 'Well, you certainly can't go yet' and when it was clear that I was determined to go in any case, she was understandably irritated and made it clear what she thought of me for forcing an extra workload on her without word of explanation or warning.

Probably she did guess something, because Warsaw was throbbing with rumours and it was clear that something mighty was about to erupt. What was less clear was the form things were going to take.

The 'readiness' order meant that every AK member had to go to his appointed place to await further instructions. In my case this meant the pharmacy in Pulawska Street. The order also stipulated that we should prepare ourselves with sufficient food and clothing for three days.

After my awkward conversation with Sophia I hurried back to my bedsit and started to get out all the carefully hoarded bits of medical equipment Wlodek and I had been saving. I went to find Hanka, and told her I was going away for a bit — again there was no question of giving any further details, nor any real need to do so — and asked her if she would look after some things for me.

She came and sat with me while I packed. As I sorted my clothes, choosing a comfortable jacket and my strongest pair of shoes, she sat on the bed and made me a good stack of cigarettes. I can see her now — sitting there, filling them on the little machine, and both of us talking as I stacked my equipment and clothes into a rucksack along with some bits of food. I was trying to be calm, soldierly and organised — inwardly I was pounding with excitement. I handed her my particularly personal letters and photographs and said that if I didn't come back she was to destroy them. I also entrusted to her care one item I specially valued — a prayer-book my mother had given me with its loving dedication on the front page in her familiar handwriting.

Then we hugged and said goodbye — she went off to her room and I was left alone in mine. It was an exciting moment. The great climax of the war, the liberation of our capital city, was about to start. I pinned on to my underclothes, beneath my blouse, the medal of Our Lady of Czestochowa[2] that I had been given when I had been formally initiated into the Sodality of Our Lady back before the war. Czestochowa is Poland's most sacred shrine, the national symbol of our commitment to Christ. Throughout the war years, devotion to the message of Czestochowa had been intense and had a renewed meaning and purpose. I was to wear this medal through everything that was to follow − it is still with me as I write this.

Among my packed clothes was the armband of white and red, stamped with the AK's official mark, which constituted my only uniform. I had to keep it firmly out of sight until the order came to put it on.

I felt bad that I couldn't say goodbye properly to Sister Stanislawa, but it wasn't possible − there just wasn't time.

Leaving my room and shutting the door behind me didn't seem particularly dramatic at the time − I was simply caught up in the excitement of what was going to happen. But it closed a chapter of my life, just as dashing off to catch the train to Warsaw when I cut short my holiday in 1939 had closed the pre-war chapter in that hot summer five years before.

Wlodek was waiting at the pharmacy, and we were joined by the two girls who completed our small unit. Wlodek made the introductions and we all shook hands rather nervously. Krysta was a slim blonde girl, her long fair hair worn in a gleaming plait around her head, and large eyes alert in her face. Ada was taller, with dark hair, slim legs, and an indefinable air of elegance and good breeding. They had been trained at the regular sessions which had been going on all over Warsaw.

The mood was tense and military: none of us made any social chat. We quickly realised that in one of the flats above us a group of our AK soldiers was similarly gathering − clearly the whole building was going to be a stronghold.

All over Warsaw people were gathering together, waiting for the final word that would send them into action. There was a breathless excitement over everything. The city was tingling with it: an air of expectancy, of gripping, poised anticipation.

A messenger arrived to say that 'W' hour — the initial had been chosen because it is the first letter of the Polish word for 'explosion' — would be a while yet. We were to remain at readiness and wait for instructions.

We talked about what we should do, and decided to seize the opportunity of getting some more food. All of us had brought what we could, but it wasn't much. We really needed some more bread, and I volunteered to go back and get some from the nuns.

When I hurried there and saw Sister Stanislawa I was really glad that I had taken this chance of saying a proper goodbye. We had always got on extremely well, and now she treated me with real affection. Of course I couldn't tell her anything — again, it was a case of 'I'm leaving, Sister — I don't know when I'll be back' — but the look in her eyes told me that she knew. Indeed, by this time all Warsaw knew. Every able-bodied young man and woman seemed to be on the move, scurrying about the city contributing to the action, the tension, and the expectancy. Sister and I looked straight at one another and there was no need for me to spell out anything in words. We embraced each other warmly and in time-honoured Polish fashion she lifted her hand to my forehead and traced the Sign of the Cross on it, as Mother had done when Janek went off to fight in 1939.

As I walked down the stairs clutching the big loaf of good-smelling bread that the nuns had given me, I was taken by surprise. My uncle — Uncle Zbigniew, who had looked in from time to time to say hello when I was working — had suddenly arrived. 'Oh — Uncle! Er . . . how nice to see you!' But this was most definitely *not* a suitable time for a social call. 'Look, I can't stop at the moment —' 'That's all right — I'll walk along with you a little way and we can talk as we go.' The look on his face, the gentleness in his tone, told me that he, too, knew what was going on and had called to say good-bye. I was grateful for this last special word with him, and we walked along together talking before exchanging warm hugs and farewell messages.

The distance between Nowogrodzka and Pulawska Street

was a longish one, and not on a tram route. The city's weird, breathless atmosphere was growing more tense by the hour, and I was part of it. As I hurried along, I could sense its tingling anticipation with every part of me. Everywhere, on every face and in every hurrying bunch of people, there was this electric mood — if anyone had tried to hold us all back and cancel the plans during the last hours he would have had a hard time of it.[3]

Where I crossed a tram route I saw that every vehicle was unbelievably crowded. It was all people could do just to grab on to the back where everyone hung on for dear life as the thing hurtled through the crowded streets.

That night our little team slept, rather uncomfortably, on the floor of the pharmacy. There was still no word of an order to move into action. The next morning brought an alarm of a different sort. The young boys in the flat above the shop — AK soldiers — acted clumsily when answering the door to a woman who had come delivering milk. When they heard her knock, they didn't know what to do, and suspected that it might be a German soldier, so they opened the door just a crack so that one of the boys could peep out, covering himself with a revolver. The woman caught sight of the gun and shrieked. Since there were Volksdeutch people living in one of the other nearby flats, who could well have heard her, we all had to flee or risk discovery. In AK parlance, the place was now 'burned out' and we would have to find somewhere else. We sent a message up the line to this effect, and got back orders directing us to a house in Mokotow, out in the suburbs. We were told we must return to the chemist's shop on Monday, and this was Saturday.

We didn't travel together, but made our way separately to the place — which turned out to be a smart villa — all reaching it at different stages of the morning. The boys upstairs were sent off somewhere else. A couple of armed AK soldiers from our regiment were detailed to provide security cover for us and accompanied us to our new post.

Now there was nothing to do but wait — we knew we'd got a sudden breathing-space. We divided ourselves into two teams for sentry-duty to keep watch. This didn't mean formally marching up and down but sentry-duty as the secret army had long known it, which consisted of walking along, apparently casually, keeping alert for anything that might threaten the hide-out. We allocated three hours on, three hours off, for this duty.

An order came asking for a messenger to carry a despatch to an address in Marszalkowska Street. Their preference was for a girl and so I volunteered and was given the envelope. When I arrived the door of the apartment was ajar. I entered and a man was sitting at a desk. He acknowledged my salute and took the envelope, read the contents and told me there was no reply. We exchanged salutes again and I sped off. I shall never know what the despatches contained, but it was obviously connected with last-minute orders for the Rising. I know now that this man was our Colonel. He was to be killed later in the Rising.

When I got back the others were brewing up some ersatz coffee. How strange it was to be spending the last tense hours before the Rising in a smartly-furnished villa. The house conveyed a general air of middle-class affluence and comfort. There was even a piano. The original owners were, of course, unknown to us — deported, perhaps, or in hiding. How the AK came to acquire the place I have no idea.

We brewed up the hot drink for ourselves and drew together in the sitting-room. How weird it all felt. I went to the piano. It was a good one and I started to play some Polish songs. Soon we were all joining in ... one song followed another, the music dispelling some of our fears and helping to untie the tight knots in our stomachs. Wlodek had a fine singing voice and could also whistle very well. Into the long summer evenings of that memorable Saturday and Sunday we sang. When the 'police hour', the curfew, came, and we could no longer post sentries, we drew the curtains and the music soared anew. We were all young, and although the next few days were — we hoped — to see the climax of all that we had been working towards for a long while, we were apprehensive and tense. A big question-mark hung over the future of all of us and all our friends. Did our army have enough guns and ammunition? Could we really hope to achieve the breakthrough over the departing Germans?

Our songs came from our very souls and echoed our deepest fears and feelings.

On Saturday and Sunday night we slept – or, rather, dozed – on armchairs or on the floor. On Monday the word came to return. From now on the hours ticked away to Warsaw's destiny. We made our way back individually to Pulawska Street, to spend the day getting everything ready. When I arrived the two pharmacists who worked there, were acting as if everything were normal. Dressed in their white coats they busied themselves behind the counter. The shop was open. We exchanged only a few words as I made my way to the room at the back. Then – just after midday – they took off, perhaps nominally for the ordinary lunch-hour, but really because everyone knew what was about to start. They were obviously in on the secret because of the way they accepted us being there without asking any questions. Probably they were in the AK too and had their own posts to reach – or perhaps they were just hurrying home to be with their families and protect them.

On Tuesday as it drew nearer and nearer to 5pm which we now knew was the hour the Rising was to begin, the tension became almost unbearable. Fear and anxiety were mingled with a sort of relief, that after the long years of misery under the Germans we were at last about to strike a blow for freedom. We had the supreme confidence of youth – deep down we hoped all would work out well.

At about half past four we heard distant firing. We were at the back of the pharmacy, where there were two rooms, a smallish one and a larger one. The shop faced on to Pulawska Street, and at the back it was part of a big apartment block, the main entrance of which also opened out on to the street. At this main entrance was a large gate, with a small door let into it. At the sound of firing, the caretaker of the block immediately rushed to shut the gate, and there were shouts and sounds of confusion as everyone began to realise that something big was happening. Shutting the gate sealed us off – we were now stuck here to face whatever fate lay ahead of us.

We wondered what had happened, and why everything had started earlier than it should have done. The noise got louder and nearer. We kept watch from the edges of the windows. Looking around the heavy blackout curtains, which had immediately been drawn, we could not see much and could only speculate as to how the battle was going. Everyone in the block was also keeping well out of sight. Most had probably fled to the basements.

We were desperate to know what was happening. Had the Rising come to a halt? We wanted to make contact with our nearest AK base. Krysta, who spoke a little German, volunteered to get out into the street and find out what she could.

Quickly she slipped out through the street door at the side of the pharmacy, where a German sentry was standing. She begged him to let her run to the next street, babbling a story about her sick mother stranded there — but he cut her short, shouting at her 'You can go, if you want to end up like that —' pointing to the dead body of a woman slumped in the centre of the road. She came back and told us it was hopeless.

From our watching-point behind the curtains we now saw German soldiers coming up the other side of the street: one behind the other, warily, Indian-file, peering all around them, with guns at the ready. We knew in a flash that we were surrounded, unable to reach any of our own troops or the territory they had captured except via the cellar routes.

As soon as dusk fell we scrambled up to the top floor of the block, a garret where curved dormer windows gave a panoramic view of the nearby square and surrounding streets. Our block overlooked the Plac Unii Lubelskiej, a roundabout named in honour of the 17th century union between Poland and Lithuania. Pulawska Street led into this, and several streets led off, including Szucha Street where the Gestapo had their headquarters, and Marzalkowska Street, which led on to a further square where stood the Church of the Redeemer with its distinctive towers. We could see buildings burning all around us, beyond the Church of the Redeemer and also in the other directions.

The next morning brought us our first wounded — two men came through the courtyard of the apartment block carrying another on a stretcher. They had made their way to us through the cellars − breaking down the internal walls from neighbouring buildings − because it was not now possible to go into the open streets. We were in action as a first-aid post.

On Wednesday night we knew that Warsaw was in flames. We scrambled up to the garret again to see if we could get any idea of what was going on. The sense of being completely cut off was terrifying.

So far we had been able to treat the two wounded who had been brought to us because they had only arm and leg injuries which were not beyond our equipment or resources. But on Thursday our third patient arrived and presented a much more serious problem. As soon as the stretcher was brought in we could see that this was something that needed an emergency operation. He had an appalling wound − his whole stomach had been ripped open. We were simply not equipped to deal with such an injury. We put on a temporary dressing, gave him something for the pain, and sent back an urgent message that he needed to be taken to hospital immediately. The Warsaw Institute of Hygiene in Chocimska Street, just round at the back of us, was meant to be the base hospital for our sector and all cases requiring surgery were meant to go there. That had been part of our instructions at the final briefing. As we waited to find out if there was any way we could get him there, Wlodek grimly made preparations for the only alternative, which was an operation in our little pharmacy with its cramped space and limited equipment.

Then, keeping watch at the windows, we suddenly saw the white-coated figure of a doctor, walking openly down the street, bearing a white flag with a red cross on it. He was accompanied by two nurses. I don't know how he managed to persuade the Germans to let him do it, but he took the badly wounded boy away. He had obviously been given some sort of pass to get down the street, and he warned us that he would not be able to come again: he thought the Germans were steadily clearing each block down Pulawska Street, one by one. All he could do was take our wounded away and wish us the best of luck. We prepared the boy very quickly for what was clearly going to be a rough journey back, and he was carried off.

Throughout the day we heard firing and shouting, smelt burning — a terrible smell — and knew that a battle was raging. The scene we saw from the garret that night was like something out of Dante's inferno.

The Germans had set fire to several blocks, and now the flames leapt upwards with a great roaring and crackling sound. We saw people throw themselves out of windows on ropes made of sheets or blankets tied together, desperate to escape from their burning homes. The figures lurched and swayed in the orange glow, trying to reach the ground. Then there was a sudden burst of machine-gun fire and some of them dropped to the ground, dead. This happened again and again. Screams rent the air, mixing with the roar of the flames and the clatter of the machine-gun fire.

What we were witnessing was not a battle but a massacre of innocent people. Cut off and unarmed, we had to view this grisly scene knowing that we could do nothing. Indeed we knew that we might be the Germans' next victims. The Jesuit church in Rakowiecka Street where I knew some of the priests, was among the burning buildings.

Everywhere, German reinforcements were in evidence. The soldiers we had seen retreating in those days before the Rising had all too clearly been replaced with fresh troops ready for a fight.[4]

Over the next day and night, still sealed off, we kept trying to make different plans. The Germans in the street could not know that we were part of the AK. We eventually decided that if they entered our block to clear it of all its inhabitants we would simply pass ourselves off as ordinary citizens — and then make a break for the nearest AK unit if we could. By this time we were in complete despair. It seemed as if everything was lost. Our story to the Germans would be that we had simply gone into the chemist's shop and got trapped there by the fighting. There were probably other people in the block who were genuinely in that position.

Just after we had put the first part of this plan into operation — hiding all our equipment in bags in the cellar and flushing our armbands down the lavatory — soldiers in German uniform burst into the shop. They grabbed us and pushed us up against the wall, and hauled off anything of value we had on us. They ripped off my little ring and my watch and grabbed my cigarette case. As they shouted and pushed us about, we quickly realised that they were not Germans but Ukrainians. Their Polish had that distinctive accent and they had special insignia on their uniforms. Many Ukrainians were by that time serving in the German army, following the German push eastwards into Ukrainian territory.

What happened next is so vivid that I see it all in a series of flashbacks.

We three girls were separated from Wlodek as the soldiers dragged him off. It became only too clear what these bullies planned to do with us next. They kept urging us to show them the way down to the cellars − just us girls. We knew this meant rape so we resisted with all the force we could muster. We were also frightened that if they got down to the cellars they would find all our AK medical equipment. It was a tense battle of wills. Then they changed tack, and pushing us from behind with their rifle-butts they shoved us out into the street.

Evidently they had been ordered to clear the whole block quickly but wanted to grab what they could before doing so. Now, a little thwarted but still richer by our watches and other items they were belatedly carrying out their instructions.

Wlodek was hauled away from us and forced in front about fifty yards away under armed guard, to be put with the other men while we were kept back with the women and children who had been dragged out of all the other houses on Pulawska Street. We were at the front of this crowd of women, as our block, being on the corner next to Unia Lubelska Place, had been the last to be emptied. Wlodek was at the rear of the group of men. As he was pushed across Unia Lubelska Place he managed to turn for a moment and half-raise his arm in a gesture of salute and goodbye.

I think he knew what was going to happen, because his face had a grey, blank look − the look of someone who realises he is on the point of death. I have never forgotten it.

The Germans now started to push all the women forward, and we were forced at gunpoint across Unia Lubelska towards Szucha Avenue, where the Gestapo building stood. Our feet crunched and slithered on thick layers of broken glass, shattered by the fighting. Szucha Avenue was a wide road, with grass verges. The Gestapo building had been protected by its occupants with sandbags and barbed wire and was so far undamaged by the fighting. This was where our men were being taken.

Krysta, Ada, and I were pushed with the other women in front of the building with the Germans herding us together all the time. Children were sobbing and holding onto their mothers' skirts, babies were screaming, and a fierce unrelenting sun was burning down on the horrific scene. Guards trained their guns on us so that no one could escape. As the waiting mounted in the heat, people began to beg for water − but the guards ignored them. Others were desperate to go to the lavatory − but no provision was made for that either. We were simply penned there as the August sun glared down − and then over the noise we heard the clatter of machine-gun fire from the inner courtyard. We had all heard this far too often during the years of occupation to mistake the sound of an execution. Shouts and screams went up from the listening women and their children. The shooting went on and on − we surged forward but could do nothing and had to hear our men being gunned down. I knew that Wlodek, with his singing and his whistling, his medical skills and his patient planning for the Rising, was dead.

I was pushing about in the crowd, trying to find out what was going on. I saw one girl I recognised − she was one of my pupil nurses at the children's home. I asked her if she had any idea of what was happening. I was desperate to know the fate of everyone in *Jelen*, and to find out what fighting there had been. Holed up in the block in Pulawska Street for the past week none of us had any idea of what had been going on. I knew that Janek's post for the launch of the Rising had been in Flora Street or in the Allee of the

Roses. Where was he now, was he still alive? Her face was grim as she tried to give me a picture of what she knew: the Germans had taken most of Flora Street and had been going into all the buildings and setting fire to the cellars — mostly by tossing in hand-grenades — before any people had time to escape. Many of the wounded were being sheltered there. It was probable that Janek had been among them.

It seemed as if there was no hope. The Germans were completely in control and were simply hunting down the Polish resistance building by building. I let the cold sick thought sink into my brain: Janek, my brother, was dead.

We were crammed partly in the street and partly on the grass verges, taking up the whole area in front of the Gestapo building, going up to Plac Unia Lubelska. We were penned there for what seemed ages, and with the desperate picture which had emerged of what had been happening, I felt that every hope had been lost and the long-planned Rising utterly crushed.

Then a tall officer appeared at the Gestapo door. At his heels there trotted a vast Alsatian dog. His hand went down to caress the animal's neck. In a loud authoritative voice he began to address us in harshly-accented Polish. He announced that a group of 'Polish bandits' had seized the postal and communication centre 'Little Pasta'. The Germans were going to go in, and we would go with them to help clear the way. The aim, he said, was simply 'to fetch our German wounded and dead'.

'Little Pasta' — the name came from running together the initials of the various postal services based there — was an important strategic objective and the German officer's first words gave me a sudden surge of hope. Our AK forces were still fighting! The battle wasn't over! In a flash, the whole scene changed, with the possibility that the Rising hadn't been wholly crushed, and there was still time to join in the fight. All was not lost ...

I could see that for Ada and Krysta the reaction was the same. The knowledge that there were Polish forces holding out gave us fresh courage and changed everything.

The Gestapo officer was still shouting, giving orders. We were to form up exactly as instructed, not look back once, and move as directed. Most of the women present broke out into fresh protests as the German soldiers moved in among us, pushing forward the younger ones and forcing us into lines ten abreast. Children became separated from their mothers, and heart-rending cries rose up.

Krysta, Ada, and I, sticking together, were pushed into a line with seven other girls. There was shouting and jostling from our guards as ranks were roughly formed. Then a tank came round from the rear of the building, and we saw what the Germans had in mind for us.

There was to be a group of two hundred women, then a tank with some women jammed on top of it, then another group of two hundred, and so on. There were three tanks in all, and the whole arrangement was stretched out across the middle of the street. Suddenly it dawned on me what the Germans were planning. We were to be used as hostages. As the tanks started to roll forward, we would be in front. The Polish soldiers would not fire on their own people, and so the Germans would be able to crush the barricades with impunity.

All around me was chaos. Many of the women had started to protest vehemently. The Gestapo officer strutted back and forth, shouting orders to his men. With one hand he directed the scene while with the other he affectionately caressed the thick glossy neck of the dog.

One little boy, no more than eighteen months or two years old, refused to be separated from his mother, and cried and screamed. He tugged at his mother's skirt, struggling to remain with her. The mother, pleading, clutched on to him as his little hands refused to let go of her dress. The tall officer reached down, picked up the child by the scruff of the neck and wrenched him from the mother's grasp. With one swift sickening movement he swung the little boy round and dashed him to the ground, where he fell with a cracking sound and lay still. The mother's struggles and cries, and those of the other onlookers, were lost in the general uproar. Meanwhile the officer's hand had crept back to the dog's neck and he had begun once more the gentle, affectionate stroking.

Now some of our guards got in amongst us, and grabbed

at bits of our clothing – a scarf here, a jacket there. They forced their arms into the jacket sleeves, often tearing them, and tied the scarves grotesquely over their helmets. They were camouflaging themselves so that they could merge with us and march alongside us to make sure none of us escaped as the whole macabre scene rolled forward, and so that they could shoot at our Polish soldiers as soon as they caught sight of them.

Krysta, Ada, and I were in the second to last rank in front of the first tank. The soldiers kept shouting at us not to look back. The tank seemed to be almost on our heels ...

As it moved forward, down Szucha Avenue, forcing us to march ahead of it, an eerie silence fell. In place of the sobs of terrified children, the only sound now to be heard was the rumble and roar of the tanks. My heart was pounding. I started to say the *Confiteor*, the ancient prayer for forgiveness and mercy in the presence of God. I was almost sure that in the next moment I would be meeting Him face to face ...

We turned into Ujazdowskie Avenue (Aleje Ujazdowskie) with the park on our right and the various villas including stately Embassy buildings on the left. This was the sector of the City that during all the years of occupation had been strictly 'Nur fur Deutche'.

We were heading down towards Pius XI Street[5] which crossed the Avenue. Ujazdowskie Avenue had always been Warsaw's smartest street, our Champs Elysées.

'Confiteor Deo omnipotente ...' As my mind jerked out the prayer we were all also looking to the left and right, alert for any sound of firing. All down Ujazdowskie Avenue only German soldiers were to be seen. We marched, tramp, tramp, tramp, down the wide street with the tank on our heels .... We swung left into Pius XI Street – and suddenly firing broke out over our heads. In this street there were buildings on both sides. The left-hand side was held by the Germans – we could see their helmets sticking up at the windows, the grey uniforms darting about. But in the windows of the blocks on the opposite side we saw our boys – the bare heads of our Polish soldiers!

Petrol bombs – 'Molotov cocktails' made from bottles filled with petrol with burning rags protruding – flew over our heads. Some of the women started to shout 'Don't shoot! We're Polish! Don't shoot!' Furious with them, Krysta and Ada and I linked arms. The German orders had been to wave white handkerchiefs, but there was no way we were going to have any part in that. Now that we had seen our AK boys we wanted to get to them. We weren't going to be helpless victims meekly obeying orders from the enemy and telling our own side not to shoot ... And now, ahead of us, we saw the barricade. It had been thrown up across the street, made of whatever materials had been to hand: pavement slabs, furniture, boards, rubble of all kinds. It stretched from one side to the other, and beyond it lay the area that was Polish territory. As we continued to march forward, the steady tramp of our feet carrying us almost unwittingly, more firing broke out and something hurtled behind us, heading for the tank.

Suddenly I saw that there was a tiny gap, between the barricade and the buildings wide enough for just one person. With arms linked, and shouting 'Run! Run!' we headed for this tiny passageway, urging forward all the girls in our rank and hurrying them along with us. Behind us as we fled we heard an almighty roar – something had caught the tank and it was going up in flames.

I still don't know how so many of us managed to cram through that tiny gap beside the barricade. One by one we hurtled through with superhuman speed. Later I was to discover that the women jammed on top of the tank had jumped down just in time and that nearly all of us in that group of two hundred had managed to get away.

On the other side of the barricade, we kept on running, down the street and towards the junction with Mokotowska. Every house was hung with Polish flags. The first entrance to a block of flats that we passed was closed, but in the next the door in the big gateway was open and as we ran toward it the people from the inner courtyard ran out to greet us. We were in free Poland! Here was our Warsaw, captured from the enemy by our own troops and held by them, separated from the invader by just one barricade and a line of AK soldiers.[6] People were reaching out to us, pulling us in, urging us to take cover from the battle raging behind us.

NOTES

Chapter 8

1. Norman Davies sums up the timing of the Rising in *Heart of Europe: A Short History of Poland* (Oxford Univ. Press, 1986): 'In July 1944, in the flood of that same offensive which brought the PKWN to Lublin and the leading units of the Soviet Army to the banks of the Vistula, General Bor-Komorowski, the AK Commander, was weighing the pros and cons of the most tragic Polish decision of the War. He knew that everyone amongst his advisers wanted the capital city to be liberated by Polish military action, and that everyone wanted to see the liberated city in the hands of an administration loyal to the Polish Government. He also knew, in the atmosphere of suppressed excitement, that the citizens might rise against the hated Germans of their own accord. So it all turned on the timing. If he gave the order too soon, the Germans would still have the strength to crush the Rising regardless. If he gave the order too late, the Soviets would enter Warsaw unopposed, and would install the PKWN on the coat-tails of their own victory parade. The only moment for a successful Rising would lie in the short interval of two or three days, after a new Soviet advance had committed the German garrison to withdraw but before the advancing Soviet troops had actually arrived in strength. On 20 July, news of the attempt to assassinate Hitler in his headquarters at Rastenburg in nearby East Prussia suggested that the *Wehrmacht* was cracking; and the evacuation of German civilian offices in Warsaw seemed to signal the start of their retreat. On the 19th, Moscow Radio broadcast an appeal urging the Varsovians to rise. A Soviet armoured division crossed the Vistula and set up a bridgehead at Magnuszew forty miles to the south. On the 31st, when a patrol of T34 tanks was sighted from Praga, in the eastern suburbs of the capital, it seemed inconceivable that the decisive moment had not arrived. At 5.30 pm Bor-Komorowski gave the order: 'Tomorrow at 17.00 hours you will start Operation Tempest in Warsaw.' A detailed analysis of the

timing is given in J.K. Zawodny's *Nothing but Honour* (New York, 1977).

2. Czestochowa is the shrine of the Black Madonna, also called Our Lady of Jasna Gora. There is a legend that the picture of Mary and her Son was painted by St Luke on a table-top made by Christ Himself when He was a young apprentice carpenter. A great church to house the shrine was built in the 15th century. Jan Sobieski, the Polish king who led the Christian forces against those of Islam in the 17th century dedicated his troops there before the start of his campaign. Poles have always believed that the shrine's history is bound up with that of their nation.

3. That evening, as General Bor-Komorowski recalls in *The Secret Army*, the Soviet Army, then heading towards the Vistula, made a dramatic radio appeal to the city: 'No doubt Warsaw already hears the guns of the battle which are soon to bring her liberation. Those who have never bowed their heads to the Hitlerite power will again, as in 1939, join battle against the Germans, this time for decisive action. The Polish Army, now entering Polish territory, trained in the USSR, is now joined to the People's Army to form the corps of the Polish Armed Forces, the armed core of our nation in its struggle for independence. Its ranks will be joined tomorrow by the sons of Warsaw. They will, together with the Allied Army, pursue the enemy westward, drive the Hitlerite vermin from the Polish land, and strike a mortal blow for the last of Prussian imperialism. For Warsaw, which did not yield, but fought on, the hour of action has arrived. The Germans will no doubt try to defend themselves in Warsaw and add new destruction and more thousands of victims. Our houses and parks, our bridges and railway stations, our factories and our public buildings will be turned into defence positions ... It is therefore a hundred times more necessary than ever to remember that in the flood of Hitlerite destruction all is lost that is not saved, that by direct action in the streets of Warsaw, in its houses, factories and stores, we not only hasten the moment of final liberation but also save the nation's property and the lives of our brothers.'

4. Norman Davies writes in *Heart of Europe: A Short History of Poland*: 'Even as the AK were taking their guns from their hiding-places, and gathering in cellars and warehouses, the German Ninth Army was moving across the Vistula bridges to launch a counter-attack against the Soviets. The German

garrison in Warsaw was strengthened by the dispatch of the SS *Viking* Panzer Division, the SS *Herman Goering* regiment, by units of military police, and by the infamous Dirlanger and RONA Brigades. This force, commanded by General von dem Bach-Zalewski and containing a strong admixture of penal battalions, convicts, and desperate ex-Soviet volunteers, was given the chance of smashing the Rising in isolation.'

5. This was named after Pope Pius XI who, as Papal Nuncio in Poland in 1920 had given considerable moral support to the Poles during the Polish-Bolshevik conflict which culminated in the 'miracle on the Vistula' when the Bolsheviks were turned back at Warsaw and the new Polish republic was established on a sound footing. The street had originally been named Piekna Street and after World War II, under Soviet domination of the country, reverted to this name.

6. The use of hostages in front of tanks was reported to London by the AK and was later mentioned by Churchill in a memorandum to Roosevelt about the Rising: 'When the Germans were bringing supplies by tanks to one of their outposts they drove before them 500 women and children to prevent the troops of the AK from taking action against them. Many of them were killed and wounded. The same kind of action has been reported from many other parts of the city.' (quoted in Churchill's war memoirs).

Chapter Nine

I cannot remember exactly what happened next, except that we were led to a basement, where there were wooden benches and tables. I think we were given something to drink — perhaps some ersatz tea or coffee? There were lots of people asking questions. This was my first glimpse of that unique life we were all to come to know in the Rising — of everyone in a block living together, like one big family. No one could stay in their own flats any more — everyone had taken to the basements, to gain some protection from the bombing and firing. They had brought with them whatever they could carry in the way of bedding, household goods, clothes and food. People were sharing what they had with one another. There were no desperate shortages as yet and everyone was happy to give to AK soldiers. Something quite unique in spirit and atmosphere was being born — although I was not in a state to be aware of it or to be conscious of anything except a pounding, throbbing sense of being alive, of being safe.

All sorts of people were crowded into that basement — old folk and young children, mothers with new-born babies, the frightened, the brave, the confused, the ill. Some people had just happened to be visiting friends or relations in a particular block when the fighting broke out and were then trapped there, cut off from their own home by the battle-lines.

In this block, fronting on to Mokotowska, people had by now been living this communual life for almost a week. It was part of a small enclave that was a stronghold of the AK, although only a matter of yards away from the German enemy.

I don't know what happened to the crowd of girls who

had escaped with us through the barricade. Everyone had simply fled to the nearest building for shelter, hurtling to safety wherever it could be found. With the first tank immobilised, all the 200 hostages just scattered, some probably being caught in the cross-fire while others, like us, found a refuge. The rest of the women and the other two tanks were turned back, and maybe the women were used again as hostages elsewhere. I was to discover later that the battle in Pius XI Street and the failure of the Germans to break through the barricade to Little Pasta was one of the major strategic incidents in the first week of the Rising in this part of Warsaw (Srodmiescie Poludnie).

As soon as we were able to do so, Krysta and Ada and I made it clear that we had to see the AK district commander, and eventually we were taken to him. He questioned us closely, first together and then individually — and initially with some disbelief about our story. As the picture emerged of what had happened, his excitement and interest mounted.

We began to realise that we were the centre of attention. The burned-out tank up against the barricade was already the talk of everyone. Our biggest surprise was to find, as our interview with the commander ended, a reporter and photographer waiting for us! They introduced themselves as being from the AK newspaper that was now being circulated regularly in the free areas of fighting Warsaw. We realised that we had found a complete Polish stronghold here, with everything functioning according to detailed plans laid down during all the months and years of patient work and planning for this Rising.

Our commander wanted every scrap of information about German troop strengths, movements, and reinforcements. How many Germans had we seen in Pulawska Street? Where were they going? All we could do was describe what we had seen: the single file of soldiers moving warily past our hide-out earlier in the week, and the tactic of using women as hostages before tanks. We wished we could bring more encouraging news — but our view had been so limited and in any case things were changing all the time.

Once convinced that we were truly AK nurses — which

entailed sending off messages to double-check, giving us a glimpse of how organised everything was here in Polish-occupied Warsaw — our commander swiftly arranged for our appointment to a new posting. We were badly needed. Now the word had got around about what had happened we were being warmly welcomed. People not only wanted to hear about our semi-miraculous escape from in front of the tanks, but were rejoicing because we were medical personnel and vitally necessary. The fighting was stepping up and trained nurses were like manna from heaven. There was dismay when it became clear that we had brought no equipment with us. There had been no moment to spare a thought for this before, but now I mourned the beautiful stack of things left behind in Pulawska Street — all the bandages and drugs and syringes, sterilised needles and proper dressings. All the things that Wlodek had so patiently collected.

Our new first-aid post was on the ground floor in what had, until a few days ago, been a café. It was properly organised and had obviously been fully planned, as had our original base in Pulawska Street. The main room, which had the big counter from which food and drinks had been served, had been turned into an operating theatre. The two rooms beyond were clinics and a dispensary. Here the 'walking wounded' were treated, while in an adjoining block rooms were filled with beds for the more serious cases. The nurses were divided into two groups — one to work in the first-aid post and the other with the bed-ridden patients. I was to be in charge of the former.

The cafe fronted on to Krucza Street, and this was perhaps the strangest thing in a day full of strange and weird experiences. I knew this particular block very well — it was part of my earliest childhood memories. My grandfather had had an apartment here, almost immediately opposite the rooms where I was now to live and work. As a little girl I had come here to live with a friend of my mother, and I vividly remembered setting off to school in the mornings, accompanied by the janitor who was in charge of all the flats.

As the recognition hit me, I felt moved and excited that I should now be living here again, this time in what were

Before the summer ended: with the Marian Sodality youth group summer of 1939.

Graduating from Warsaw School of Nursing, 1943:
with our lecturer in anatomy and physiology.

With Halszka, friends and posies.

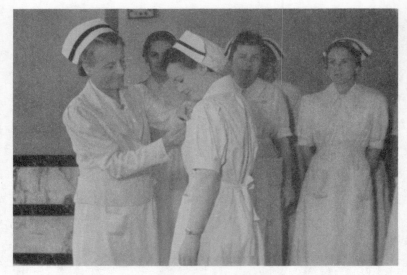

The Principal of Warsaw School of Nursing pins on my nurse's badge.

Receiving congratulations.

After liberation from the prison camp — with my brother on the road to Italy. I'm wearing the vast US Army greatcoat.

In uniform, Italy, 1946.

In Italy, 1946.

Meeting General Anders with the 7th Polish Lancers on the
Regimental Feast Day, Italy 1946.

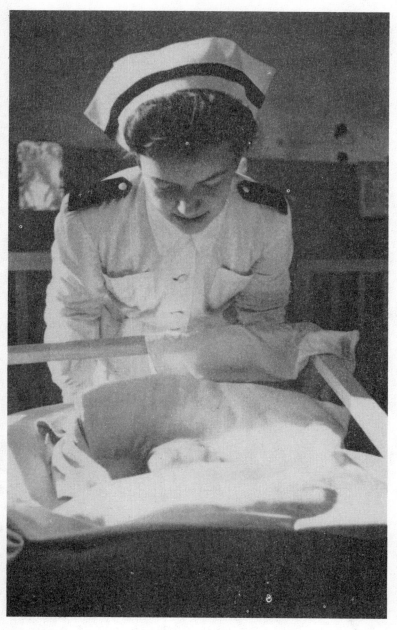

The Children's Ward,
Polish Military Hospital No. 340, Trani, Italy.

Wedding portrait, 6th July 1946.

surely going to be the most stirring and exciting days of
Warsaw's history.

The work was explained to us.

The major hospital for this district was in Mokotowska
Street. Our little unit, and the rooms with beds in the next
block, were for the cases that were within our scope. Our
main work would not be only in treating the wounded who
were brought to us, but in going out and fetching them
ourselves. Stretchers, bandages, drugs and equipment were
ready and waiting − it went without saying that we would
have to be thrifty and careful in our use of every item: we
did not know how long it would be before new supplies
arrived.

In one of the rooms there were makeshift beds on which
we could sleep. We had arrived, of course, without a single
personal item − not a comb, toothbrush, change of clothes
or towel. But people were anxious to help, and we were
provided with the things we needed. There was even soap −
the normal harsh gritty stuff that we had been obtaining on
ration cards throughout the war years.

The next morning I was completely disorientated. Where
on earth was I, what had happened? Fear and bewil-
derment − a delayed reaction from the previous day −
made me lose my grip on reality. Everything seemed remote
and peculiar.

Out of this void, I tried to grasp hold of something
tangible. What day was it? It was Sunday, 6th August. I
suddenly wanted very badly to go to church. I tentatively
asked about it − and some one told me there was no need to
go anywhere, as it was all coming here, to the courtyard.

I will remember all the days of my life this unique
gathering of a battered, undefeated community on its knees
before God.

People came in twos and threes or singly: mothers leading
small children, old people with quiet courage in their faces,
AK soldiers with the grey look that comes from complete
exhaustion.

A sort of open-air church was being created, with a
cross on a table surrounded by all the flowers that could
be found.

It was the feast of the Transfiguration – the day on which the Church around the world commemorated the event described in the Gospels: when Our Lord took Peter, James, and John up to a mountain-top and was there suddenly transformed before them, shining with a heavenly light and conversing with Moses and Elias.

The chaplain's sermon drew out the message of the Gospel story, and its applications to our situation. He managed to put our feelings into his words, drawing together an understanding of the hugeness and immortality of Christ's message, and the new daily reality with which we were all faced. It was a strange coincidence: not only was this a special day in the Church's calendar, but also in Poland's – August 6th was the day, each year, when we commemorated the march of Pidsulski's legions in World War I which led to our independence.

In this communion with God we were lifted out of the stomach-gripping uncertainty about the future: what was going to happen in the next few days? Would the Allies send aeroplanes? Were the Soviets already on their way across the Vistula? Did we have enough ammunition, food, bandages, supplies? The future of each of us as individuals hung in the balance, and so did the future of our Poland, its place on the map, its claim to be a nation in its own right, the collective identity of its people. Now we all glimpsed the spiritual truth at the heart of everything.

For Krysta and Ada and me that morning was in a sense a celebration of our own transfiguration – from helpless victims hiding in a chemist's shop, or hostages forced to march in front of tanks, to people who had been given a new chance of life, and new work to do in it. In my heart the fear and disorientation were gone, replaced by a renewed commitment and faith.

I didn't want to be anywhere on earth but Warsaw – alongside my friends in the defence of our much-loved city.

At the end of Mass some one struck up a hymn and we all took it up. It was the one that we had all sung over and over again during the years of occupation, whenever people gathered together for prayer: 'Listen, Lord Jesus, hear how

your people plead to you ...' Today, the words soared up
from Polish throats to a Polish sky in a part of our capital
city won back by our own forces, and I have never forgotten
just how that felt and sounded.

Next we made our way to a big room in a neighbouring block which had been commandeered by the 'Pomoc
Zolnierzowi' or 'Support the Soldiers' women's organisation.
How we were to bless this organisation in the days ahead.
Like everything else, it had been planned down to the last
detail in the days before the Rising: the 'peżet' as it came to
be called, aimed to provide food, comforts and relaxation
for our Home Army troops when they were off-duty, and
a focal point to which everyone could go for snacks, music,
companionship and news. This big hall was to be the scene
of many gatherings in the days ahead. On this sunny Sunday
morning we enjoyed the first of them. I was soon pressed
into service at the piano. A concert programme arranged
itself spontaneously: people came forward to sing, tell jokes
or stories, recite poetry, or lead choruses.

The music held a message: that everyone was throwing in
their lot together and supporting one another. Everyone in
that hall was in a state of uncertainty: about their homes,
future, family safety, and livelihood – all the ordinary
everyday things of life. And yet the unselfish determination
not to complain, not to give way to fear or discouragement,
was magnificent – and contagious. The mood was cheerful,
optimistic, and resolute.

I feel truly sorry for anyone who has not experienced in
life something of this sense of shared adventure – of human
solidarity at its most marvellous.

We felt very much part of this community when we
reported back for duty at our first-aid post, to get things
ready for that night's action.

The café housing our dispensary was at the front of the
block. In the civilised days before the fighting – already
receding into the far distance – there would usually be a
caretaker or concierge in charge of each block. He would
answer enquiries and supervise the upkeep of the building.
The courtyards would be smart with flowers and shrubs and
the bell to each different flat would be marked with a brass

plaque giving the resident's name. In the new situation in which we found ourselves social formalities were becoming irrelevant. The whole collection of apartments was taking on the atmosphere of a walled fortress. The entrance, with its big gate with the smaller door let into it was guarded by AK soldiers, who also manned strategic windows and vantage-points looking out on to the street.

We had two doctors. One was Dr Jan, a general practitioner, and the other Dr Zygmunt, who was older and a surgeon. Dr Jan was actually a military man, serving officially with the AK, which gave him a higher rank than the surgeon, who was a civilian — an unusual reversal of the normal medical procedure. So it was Dr Jan who was in command of our little unit. He was small in stature, very quick and neat in all his movements. I was to find he was a good doctor, and a leader one could trust — a typical old-fashioned military man. Dr Zygmunt came originally from Poznan, and was a well-known surgeon. He exuded an air of solid reassurance, competence and calm, with a dignity and kindliness that were a great strength.

While I began my new work my thoughts flew for a moment to Mother and Helena and far away in Saska Kepa, on the other side of the river and Jadzia in Bielany. I wished I could let them know that I was still alive, and so far all right. I desperately wanted to find out how things were with them. They didn't yet know, had no means of knowing, about Janek. Janek — dead somewhere in a block like this, his body burned to ashes or perhaps lying decaying and unrecognisable under rubble in a basement.

I met the nurse with whom I was to work closely from now on — Wisia, who was in charge of the rooms with beds for in-patients while I took over running the first-aid post for the 'walking wounded'. She was small and slim, with wide-set eyes and long fair hair worn in two plaited coils round her ears. We shook hands. I would come to find her a good colleague — quiet, systematic and well-organised.

The word had come that a Home Army initiative was planned. We had to be realistic — we knew there would be substantial casualties and we had to prepare for them. We made ready our little operating theatre, beds and bandages.

The equipment even included white coats marked with red crosses on the sleeves for us to wear.

As darkness fell, those of us who were not directly involved with the action, found ourselves drawing together, wanting to be with each other in the time of waiting and tension.

An 'action' didn't consist of charging gloriously down a street or noisily storming a major building from the outside. Lack of ammunition, and the peculiar circumstances of the battle, combined to make that an impossible dream. An attack meant creeping stealthily through the dark, via cellars and attics, to surround the appointed place, and then capturing it relying chiefly on surprise, opening the way for the unit to move forward and consolidate the position and thus regain a very small amount of the territory lost the day before, or edge towards a desired strategic objective.

Once the fighting began in such an attack, it was savage and ferocious, but the early part meant silence and edging forward inch by inch. As we sat back at our own post, waiting, we were with our soldiers in spirit every moment of the way, and to express this and perhaps to drown out any noise they might be making, we started to sing.

The singing began from somewhere further off − far back in the block, from where the boys had gone. It was one of our own songs, the music that had become part of the AK, set against the background of Polish folklore and long-ago tales of heroism. While some sang, others hummed − and gradually more and more young voices took up the theme, and our message went up into the warm night sky: 'A soldier was walking down the road . . . ' The verses tell how a soldier took the heart of the girl he loved into battle with him, so that he was never alone, never unloved. It exactly summed up what we were trying to say. We were with the boys as they crept silently across rubble, slid into an abandoned staircase, waited breathlessly on a corner − and then surged forward with their makeshift weapons. The singing took some of the ache out of waiting, and we were ready when the wounded were brought back to us, to give of our best for them.

This was the Warsaw of which I was now a part, with the Home Army fighting in the role for which it had been training for nearly half a decade. The mood among us −

the younger ones — was exultant. It was summed up on
the posters that had appeared on the walls of the streets and
blocks we occupied: 'Do Broni!' 'To arms!' After five years
of secrecy, silence, and grim endurance it was something to
be able to talk freely about the things that really mattered,
to go about your work openly, to be fighting side-by-side
with people who shared your convictions and your loyalties.
Bullets, fires, hunger and dangers were only to be expected
in battle and we were prepared to face them. We were one
hundred per cent behind our commander, General Bor, a
man whose name was soon known by all.

Dr Zygmunt had a tremendous sense of inner calm and
peace — he never flapped even when there was chaos all
around him. Working with him you caught this mood, and
it was a great strength as we struggled to maintain cleanliness
and to cope with messy wounds with the sounds of battle in
our ears. That first night set a pattern that was to be followed
by many others.

It was within only about 48 hours of being part of this new
unit that I attended its first funeral. It was on the other side of
Mokotowska Street. A young lieutenant. The priest blessed
the ground and we said the traditional prayers commending
the boy's soul to the love and mercy of God: 'Eternal rest
grant unto him, O Lord . . . May Thy perpetual light shine
upon him . . .' We also prayed the Angelus for him, that
lovely prayer commemorating the Incarnation, with the plea
'that we may be made worthy of the promises of Christ'. We
made a cross of wood and put his name on it.

So beneath the August sun — the weather was still
scorchingly hot — the crosses were beginning to appear in
the streets and courtyards. There was no question of trying
to drag the dead out to the city cemetery, miles away across
the German lines. Where paving-stones had been pulled up
to make barricades, the soft earth was waiting — and the
dead were buried among us as we lived and fought. A
funeral brought people together, and it meant that news
from different sectors could be hurriedly exchanged: we got
a slightly broader picture of what was going on.

We started to get very tired. We slept for a bit in the early
hours of each morning — in shifts, of course, so that there

was always a nurse available. Krysta and I shared a sofa-bed, but sometimes things were too chaotic to get it organised, and the only thing available was a chair, or the floor.

For food, we relied on the '*peżet*' teams who organised cooking, and fair distribution from a central kitchen.

The '*peżet*' food was mostly soup, made from whatever was available. Working under intense pressure, we sometimes went for long periods without eating – and then were too tired for anything and collapsed on to our makeshift beds for sleep.

These days – the first fortnight of the Rising – were a time of confusion but also of great hope and optimism. Caught up in nursing the wounded I was too busy to note much of what was happening on the wider scene and like many others tended to live from day to day, or even hour to hour. We knew of certain developments. The AK newspapers, sometimes complete with photographs, told of the exploits of our Home Army, and we learned that a radio station had been set up and that we were in contact with London. This meant that our Allies knew of our battle and of our desperate need for help, and would surely be doing all they could for us. The expectation of British 'planes grew hourly, and rumours abounded.

There were developments, too, in our own small areas of hard-won territory. A postal service was started, with Scouts and Guides in charge. The youngsters, some of them teenagers, others as young as nine or ten years old, carried the letters in shoulder-bags specially made for the purpose. They ran with these to the different destinations through the cellars and into the apartment blocks, and were successful in putting large numbers of people in touch with one another.[1] I sent a letter back to Sister Stanislawa this way, and decided to go and see her if I got the chance.

Within its limits, Polish Warsaw was a complete little independent republic. But contact with anyone outside the area accessible to our Polish troops was simply impossible: the Soviets were approaching from one side of Warsaw, the Germans still held the other, and we were an island in the middle.

It wasn't even one identifiable island. Within one street,

some buildings were held by Germans and some by us. Sometimes our Home Army men could hear German voices only a few feet away on the other side of a wall. Battles were being fought for a street corner, a church, a set of shops or offices. Our hold on our own territory was dependent on limited supplies of ammunition − this was the crucial item we were seeking in the air-drops from British or Allied 'planes.

The cellars were now becoming a standard underground route. All along a street, the walls dividing the cellars of different houses had been knocked down, so that you could walk from one to the next − cautiously because of the rubble − and eventually re-emerge where you needed. The main roads were clearly marked, so that you knew you were walking down such-and-such a street, turning left and heading for a particular house. The numbers were chalked up on the walls. Teams of people were in charge of the cellars, breaking down the walls, posting up directions and providing some kind of rudimentary lighting. Some roads even had electric light − others were lit by candles or lanterns of various kinds. In others the going was tougher and you carried your own torch or simply a piece of burning wood to light your way. Again the children − Scouts and Guides − were often the experts here, and could find their way about even when the grown-ups were baffled. There was so much courage in these small faces. In the first few days, many of the youngsters proudly wore their Scout or Guide uniforms, but as time went by these got filthy and stained, and they reverted to any other clothes they could find. Washing and changing clothing, along with everything else, was getting more and more difficult, as we were all finding.

Then came the day that transformed everything for me. The boys went for an 'action' and I was sitting with Dr Zygmunt when Wisia ran in to say that two wounded had been brought in and he was needed to do some surgery at once. She wanted to borrow some instruments that properly belonged to my first-aid clinic but were needed for the operation. 'Bring them back as soon as you're finished with them,' I warned her sternly, knowing that once out of my sight these precious items might stay away for ever.

She told me that one patient had been badly wounded in the eye, but there was little time for conversation as we were both already hurrying about to deal with the other results of the night's fighting. Later when Dr Zygmunt came back I asked him − which was unusual because we didn't generally have time to exchange conversations about patients − how things had gone and he told me that the man's life was still in the balance and that if he lived it was uncertain whether the sight of the eye could be saved.

Next morning several patients arrived to have their dressings changed and I realised we would need some of the instruments Wisia had borrowed the night before, and stumped off rather angrily to get them.

'Wisia − you absolutely promised −' I began. I was standing in the small room, where the dressings and equipment were kept. It led off a corridor, and opposite was another room with two beds in it. Suddenly, from the room opposite I heard my name being called − my real name that I had not used for a long while since to everyone in the AK I was just automatically Irena.

'Cechna' − my pet name in the family, the diminutive of Cecylia. Who was calling me? I thought it must be my imagination, but it came again, and this time it was very clearly from the room where the two beds were. I ran in. One of the patients had his face half-covered in bandages, but I saw enough of it to recognise ... Janek!

Neither of us could believe it. For a split second we just stared at one another, and then I rushed towards him and dropped down on my knees beside the bed.

'I knew it was your voice, and I just called out, but I could hardly believe −' he was saying. I had been so certain that Janek was dead that it was like a miracle to have him lying there. Our news now tumbled out in a torrent of words. We found we had spent the past few days within a few streets of one another. He had not been in the cellars of the Allee of the Roses − he had been among the soldiers firing at the Germans on the day of the big battle when we were marched in front of the tanks. I realised as he told his story that he had been among those who saved my life, by covering me and the other girls as we rushed into the gap at the edge of the barricade to freedom. Then his unit had re-grouped for another series of actions, including the previous night's, in which he had been badly hurt.

His wound was very, very near his eye, and there was a big question-mark over whether he would ever see out of that eye again. But he didn't want to talk about his injuries. He wanted to know my story, and any news of what had been going on in the sector with which I had been in contact. I told him about the executions at the Gestapo headquarters, the women herded together as hostages – and the dreadful moment when I heard about the Germans using grenades to clear out cellars full of wounded men and had assumed he was dead.

We talked briefly about Mother and Helena, and speculated on what was happening to them. But our world had shrunk to our tiny patches of Polish-held territory, and Saska Kepa, where now the Soviet tanks might be in command, was as impossible to reach as if it had been a thousand miles away.

Janek's presence changed everything. From now on, all my off-duty moments, such as they were, could be spent with him. Lying in the next bed was our cousin, Valery. They had both been fighting side-by-side in the same regiment, and were now both wounded together.

I rushed off to find Dr Zygmunt, and demanded to know the exact problem with Janek's wound, and how serious it was: 'And you must be absolutely frank with me, because I've got a right to know – he's my brother!' Dr Zygmunt was amazed at this meeting of members of a family in the chaos of war and was helpful, practical and realistic in his diagnosis. I knew he would do his best for Janek and thanked God that my brother was in such good hands.

Over the next days I spent much of my free time with Janek and Valery, but I was also busy with the Pezet. Groups presented songs and sketches, and anyone who could play a musical instrument, sing or recite, or lead some communual entertaining, was needed.

Rooms in blocks as far as possible from the firing-line were chosen for these gatherings. The faces gathered together in the evening sunshine were unforgettable. We were all so strongly conscious of all that we held in common, so aware of what these critical days meant to all our futures. These concerts had a haunting dramatic quality. There would be wounded men with their bandages and slings, a few exhausted off-duty nurses with their stained and grubby clothes, young boys snatching a brief break before going off on the next patrol, anxious older people with haunted eyes and hungry faces, determined not to show fear. Our songs and poetry showed that our hopes for victory, our belief in the value of what we were doing, our longing for a time and a country where we could live together in peace, were poignantly alive.

We had been holding out now for nearly three weeks. I had originally been told to bring rations and equipment to last for three days.

NOTES

Chapter 9

1. *Nothing But Honour* by J.K. Zawodny (Macmillan, 1978) notes: 'From 6 August simple makeshift boxes appeared in territory held by insurgents, usually in the vicinity of barricades or hospitals. These were collection points. Some boxes were labelled 'Field Postal Service' but more often they were designated by a lily, the symbol of Polish Scouting. Each box was emptied twice a day, unless the postman (none was older than fifteen) was killed.'

Chapter Ten

Janek's eye was slowly healing — although it would never be quite right — and as he lay in bed we went over all our news and pieced together bit by bit how the first week of the Rising had gone, and what had been happening to all our friends during those critical days when I had been holed up in Pulawska Street.

Krystyna (Krahelska) was dead. She had been killed alongside Zbyszek, Janek's old schoolfriend. It had happened very early on in the first outbreak of fighting, when *Jelen* was struggling to wrench territory from the enemy's hands and gain its first strategic objective.

Janek told me what had happened. Zbyszek had been caught by enemy fire and slumped to the ground. Krystyna had started to run and help him. A moment later she was also gunned down, and fell within yards of where he lay. Even if she had been able to reach him, it would have been too late — he had died instantly.

While I heard of the deaths of old friends, I was also attending the funerals of new ones. We weren't able to save the life of every patient that was brought to us, and it was a bitter moment when our best efforts failed and a boy's life slipped away. You never get used to this. I had been working as a nurse for several years, in the difficult conditions of an occupied country in wartime, when precious drugs were unobtainable, and people died in greater pain than they should have done and we were powerless to help them — but the tragedies had not immunised me for the new sorrow of death on the battlefield.

Because of what I saw and shared in the Rising, I have

never been able to accept the fashionable view on euthanasia which has become popular in the years since the War. People say that those who are dying in agony long for death — that it would be a kindness to put them out of their misery. However in my experience that just isn't true. I never nursed a man who didn't cling to life, and want to live with every breath that was in him. They longed for release from pain, but not from life itself.

'Don't let me die, Sister', a man would plead. 'I don't want to die — oh, please, I don't want to die.'

This longing for life is something entirely natural — and it is a terrible thing to deny it to a man or woman.

The bravery that we saw was extraordinary, and moved us nurses profoundly. We felt we would do anything for these boys.

We were using gentian violet for the burn cases, and iodine was our basic antiseptic for wounds and abrasions. Bandages were washed and sterilised in boiling water and used again and again — nothing could be wasted. We also had considerable quantities of paper dressings — of a crepe sort that stretched out as they were pulled.

However, if we were making out all right for bandages so far, the problem of ammunition was becoming acute. The AK never had very much — our weapons consisted of some carefully hidden since the September 1939 fighting, some captured from the Germans at various stages before or during the Rising, and some sent in by the Allies. Not much was reaching us by this last method — every day our hopes were raised by the news or rumour of British planes coming in from the West bringing a desperately-needed airlift of equipment, but even when they started to fly in, many of these brave pilots were shot down and very few of their supplies actually got to us. So whole teams of people were employed in the manufacture or repair of weapons for AK use.

These included not only very simple items such as petrol bombs — just bottles filled with petrol with a rag sticking out of the top to be ignited — but also whole arsenals of more sophisticated weaponry. Nothing was allowed to go to waste. A captured German gun that had ceased to function would be stripped down and working again within 24 hours. All our carefully-hoarded items needed to be kept in full use. Every bullet, every scrap of anything remotely usable in any capacity, was precious.

An officer was working on one of these weapons teams in Koszykowa Street, producing some grenades or firearms out of whatever was available when something went horribly wrong and the whole thing suddenly exploded in his hands. A Boy Scout messenger ran to summon us and to guide us to the block where the man lay. Krysta and I picked up a stretcher and set off. We had by now learned that extra risks were incurred if we went wearing our white overalls clearly marked with the red crosses: the sight of such uniforms seemed to make the German marksmen more determined to get us. So we were in our ordinary clothes − by now a dirty and tatty mixture − as we began the journey.

Marszalkowska Street was continually changing hands between the Germans and the Poles and all the roads immediately near it were terribly vulnerable. The barricade protecting Koszykowa was the trickiest part of our trip. Once we were safely behind it we felt the worst was over.

We found the slumped unconscious body of a very badly burned man, who had hundreds of tiny coils of metal springs embedded in his flesh, covering, it seemed, every part of him. It was a horrifying sight, and his injuries were only part of the problem − our main worry was how to get him back.

The deadly threat at a barricade came from the German gunmen perched high up on neighbouring buildings, training their sights on any Pole attempting to cross. You had to be quick in order to thwart them of their prey. The tiny space between the barricade and the houses on the side of the street was wide enough for one person to slip through. The snipers shot with Germanic precision, aiming always for the head or the heart − they had obviously been chosen for this task for their skills in marksmanship.

The small Boy Scout who had led us to Major L. had shown no fear. But we could not put his young life at a greater risk than necessary. As soon as we reached the barricade with our heavy patient on the stretcher we realised that the resulting burden was far too wide to pass through the narrow gap. We sent the little boy on ahead, saying that we knew the way back, and recognising that he stood a better chance without us slowing him down. Then the two of us set the stretcher down while still within the comparative shelter of a building and had a consultation. We decided to do the only thing possible — carry it carefully over the top. This meant that for a few — it felt like a great many — terrifying moments we were completely explosed to enemy fire, sitting targets for anyone who wanted to pick off all three of us. I still don't know why we weren't killed.

We got him back, and as he was an emergency case he was taken immediately into our little operating theatre. Carefully extracting all those tiny pieces of metal turned out to be a long and nasty job. He survived, and for me became a sort of prize patient, after all the trouble we had gone through to get him. There was a tremendous satisfaction in popping in to see him at odd moments and noting that he was holding his own and steadily getting better.[1]

The Germans were calling us 'Polish bandits' but we took pride in being a proper army — an army that obeyed the honourable rules of war even when its enemy did not. A substantial number of German prisoners had now been captured, and a group were under guard near us. They were set to work clearing rubble and building barricades. How terrified they looked when they were first brought in! They were convinced, we discovered, that they would either be shot out of hand, or perhaps mercilessly tortured, as they were sure that we were an uncivilised bunch of thugs. They were pretty stunned to find that we were not like that at all, and were prepared to accord them all the proper treatment due to prisoners of war under international conventions.

They got the same as us to eat — which wasn't much, but was fairly portioned out — and it was made clear that anyone who ill-treated them would be punished. Secretly, we were amused at how obedient and submissive these prisoners were, and how willing to do almost any task required of them. Our image of haughty Germans was replaced with that of cowering, timid creatures, anxious to please and respectful of our orders.

For ourselves, our determination to act decently was

not just a matter of AK discipline, but also of Christian tradition. We even had a prayer-card specially for AK members, showing the Mother of Christ looking down on an AK soldier and covering him with her mantle.

Our dispensary acquired two further helpers at this time — one was an Azerbaijani and the other a Georgian. They were big men with jet-black hair. City life was evidently quite foreign to them, and urban warfare an experience they had never even contemplated. We never got around to asking their story or why they were with us — we all just got on with work together. There were so many different people now thrown together by the battle who felt like old friends and had been complete strangers just days before.

We were hearing radio broadcasts from London now, sometimes gathering round a set to listen. For years, people had been listening to the BBC in secret, tuning in with great difficulty to a hidden wireless set, an offence punishable by death if discovered by the Gestapo. Now we would listen openly — and we heard London reporting that Warsaw was fighting, and felt that there were people there backing us up, willing us to battle on.

Our main hope still centred on the airlifts from our allies, specifically Britain. At night everyone scanned the skies after hearing that 'planes were on the way. We talked a lot about the things we needed, and what might be brought. The main thing was simply guns and ammunition — everything else was secondary. One or two drops did now reach us — we saw the 'planes overhead and heard them, and there was a great shouting and waving as items came down on parachutes. What excitement! Suddenly morale was raised to high levels. But many of the parachute parcels fell into the streets that were held by the Germans. The map was changing day by day — to make an accurate drop must have been virtually impossible, despite the frantic signalling from the ground below.

It meant so much that we were part of the wider allied cause. And yet the radio broadcasts sometimes seemed strange to us. Again and again one particular piece of music was played — it was 'Z dymem pożarów' (With the smoke of the fires), a tragic, mournful tune which only seemed to emphasise the increasing difficulties of our situation. 'With the blood of our brothers ...' the radio would sing out, driving us crazy. We who were in the front line were cheerful and ready to face each new challenge with exhilaration — why couldn't London understand this?

Much later, after the war, I discovered that this tune was one of those used as part of a code to announce whether or not flights were on their way to us with supplies. The mournful music was only too appropriate for the code which said there would be no flights that night, and the frequency with which we heard it tells its own story. The number of planes lost by enemy fire on their way to Warsaw or over the city itself was very high, and the results from the 'planes that did get through were not very satisfactory in terms of the amounts of equipment actually received by us on the ground. A large number of brave young pilots gave their lives in these flights, not only Polish pilots flying under British command, but also other allies: Canadian, South African, American, and British. The death-rate was very high and these men had flown under dangerous conditions all the way from distant southern Italy, where the nearest British and American bases were.

The most baffling thing was the behaviour of the Soviets. Why did they appear to have halted their advance, just when they were virtually on the point of crossing the Vistula? If we could hold off the Germans for so long, with just our limited ammunition, surely they with their tanks and artillery could manage a breakthrough, with their far more sophisticated weaponry? Everything pointed to the Soviets being able to make a quick crossing, so that we could welcome them into a liberated city, saving lives and benefiting the common cause. Who was gaining anything from this delay except the Germans?

There was no rational explanation for the Soviets' failure to move forward. We expected action from them daily — and every day it didn't happen.

One afternoon I managed to make my way — via the cellar routes — out to the nursing home to find out how things were there. Sister Stanislaus was busy and so was Sophia and I could only stay a short while, but I managed to talk to one of the doctors and found out that so far everyone was surviving.

I met up with another old friend, too — Olga, whom I had last seen when we were both taking our AK nursing exams together over a year before. She was now busy running a unit similar to mine not far away and we exchanged news about how things were going.

At night when I had a few moments to spare before I went to sleep, my thoughts flew to my mother in Saska Kepa, just a short distance away across the river, from where she would be able to see the glow of the fires and hear the pounding of the guns.

Lying there in Krucza Street my thoughts went back to a childhood memory of being in a cosy bed in a corner of the room I shared with my mother, watching her walk quietly up and down, her rosary in her hands, praying as I dozed off to sleep. Sometimes she would pause and, standing by the window, would make the Sign of the Cross in one particular direction and then a bit later in another — praying for my sisters and their families, living in different parts of Poland.

It comforted me to think that perhaps she was doing that now, making the Sign of the Cross to us over the Vistula. When there was a bombardment she would see the glow in the sky from the burning buildings and know that we were somewhere in that inferno.

So many families were separated. When we were burying a boy we hadn't had time to get to know properly I would think and think about his family: his mother and father, somewhere in this barricaded city of fires and tanks and ambushes. Who were they? Were they hoping and praying that he was all right — maybe trying to send him letters?

When we knew a dead boy's name we had an identity tag made for him — beaten out of an old tin can, with his name and details punched on it. We wanted people to know, some day, where their sons or husbands lay.

However despite the gloom and hardship happier chapters of family life were also being written. I went to a wedding. There were quite a few at this time. It was inevitable, in this extraordinary atmosphere of tension, heroism and heightened emotions, that young couples in love took a quick decision and opted to be together even if life was only granted to them for a few more days.

K. and J. were one such pair. Those of us who could, scrambled to the church for the wedding. Some one had managed to find a spray of flowers for the bride — a posy of bright red geraniums from a window-box not yet shattered by the fighting. They made a splash of colour pinned to her dress, and she also had a bright ribbon threaded through her hair. The bridegroom wore uniform — or anyway, bits of it: a khaki jacket with civilian trousers. We gathered round as they made their marriage vows, and then showered them with hugs and good wishes when the brief ceremony was over. No reception, toasts, speeches or champagne — food was running far too short for that.

The traditional religious ceremonial associated with things like marriage and death had a deeper and more profound meaning in our situation, perhaps precisely because they were shorn of any outward glamour or trimmings.

Every regiment had its own chaplain, one of whose main tasks was to be with the dying. All were kept very busy. I made friends with Father Kwiecinski, a kindly priest based in Wilcza Street, in what had been a home for retired domestic servants. He never failed to come to be with a dying man, and I would run for him when our own chaplain was not available. Father Kwiecinski would hurry at once, carrying the Blessed Sacrament in a special silver box in his breast pocket, scrambling over the rubble and taking his chance at the barricades.[2]

The Church calls the last Communion of a person's life the Viaticum or 'food for a journey'. Many men were able to receive this spiritual nourishment and face death at peace with Christ because Father Kwiecinski was there to bring it to them.

Wood for crosses was getting harder to find now, and we had stopped trying to make coffins too. The bodies were just wrapped in whatever cloth was available before being gently lowered into the soil in a side-street or the courtyard of a block of flats. Sometimes we found we didn't know a dead boy's real name, only his AK alias. But the worst thing was that we couldn't bury every dead body. Sometimes people were trapped in burning or collapsing buildings, and their bodies were unreachable, pinned down by masonry. In the hot August nights and days they rotted, giving out a nauseating smell: in a big block there might be quite a number of them and the stench was sickening, indescribable.

I was beginning to feel that one by one all the young men and women of my generation were being killed off. Among those now lying beneath Warsaw were so many of the young people I had talked with, sang with, planned and hoped and endured with, during the years of Occupation and the days of fighting – people who were part of the very essence of things. Who would be alive to see the final day of liberation?

Over a month into our Rising, and even though we were unable to see the wider scene from our own corner around Mokotowska, Pius XI, and Krucza Streets, we were getting a rough picture of what was happening. A battle was raging in Stare Miasto, the Old Town, a stronghold of our forces. It had been held precariously against tremendous odds for days. But how could it withstand the constant bombardment from the new weapons that the Germans were now hurling against us?

I wanted to be alone with God. I managed to make my way to Wilcza Street. The little chapel which was Father Kwiecinski's base in the former servants' home was still intact. I went down on my knees and asked God to give me the strength, endurance and faith I needed for whatever lay ahead. Never had He seemed so near, so immediate. I was not alone in those days in being powerfully conscious of His presence, of the mysterious closeness of His crucified Son amongst us.

The new bombardment was something quite different from what we had experienced before. Evidently the Germans were despairing of ever being able to crush our barricades with tanks. They now produced this much more terrifying weapon: it was a sort of multiple-headed rocket launcher, able to fire off several massive missiles at one go. These made a strange and eerie mooing sound as they were fired: we called them 'cows'. The whining howl meant that you

knew what was coming – you sat in the basement tense
and sick with fear, and then when the crash and explosion
came and you knew you had survived for one more time,
you crawled out to begin the task of rescuing the wounded,
hunting in the rubble, burying the dead.

The bombardments produced moments of black humour.
We laughed, for instance, at the effect of the 'cows' on our
big Caucasian mountain helpers. These burly men dropped
straight to the floor, terror-stricken, at the first sound of
them, and on one occasion one snaked across the courtyard
on his hands and knees during a bombardment, to reach
shelter.

We were fighting back, and tales of our Home Army
soldiers' bravery were becoming legendary. With a desperate
shortage of ammunition they were making do with whatever
came to hand – and holding out magnificently. They knew,
too, that the whole population was with them – this was a
battle in which every Warsaw citizen was involved.

At the 'peżet' concerts this spirit came out tangibly –
everyone wanted to cheer on our soldiers, to show support
for the cause, to contribute to keeping morale high. Already,
people had given food, furniture, clothing and household
goods – sacrificing their possessions to make weapons,
barricades, or other necessities. There was a tremendous
willingness to share things and at this stage people seemed
to outdo one another in generosity and in service.

Krysta and I went along to the *pezet* hall when we had
a couple of hours off duty. Some one was singing as we
entered, and soon everyone was joining in. People presented
drama and poetry – and then voices rose again in song.
For a brief while you could forget the battles and the
bombardment, and draw strength and encouragement from
being together with people sharing the same spirit in the face
of the same difficulties.

These concerts were informal affairs, with people coming
and going as they pleased. As the concert drew to its close
and people lingered talking, we wandered over to the piano.
No sheet music was needed for the songs that were part
of our lives. I started to play one of our favourites and
Krysta perched on a nearby chair, resting her arms on the

piano-top. A soldier came up to join us — Jan, a boy we both knew well by sight and had chatted with from time to time. Tall and fair — rather handsome — he had that look that all our soldiers had, with a lean face and tired eyes very bright beneath their lashes.

The late afternoon sun filtered into the room through the cracked and broken window-panes. The last concert-goers were making their way back across the rubble. Jan's deeper voice joined mine in the song as he stood by me at the piano. We sang the one that, perhaps more than any other, was the love-song for our generation — the Markowski one about the soldier going off to war with the heart of his girl always beside him.

Jan's hand moved round on to my shoulder as we enjoyed the music, here in the embattled heart of the Poland we had promised solemnly, in front of a crucifix, to defend with our lives.

One song followed another, and for half an hour the outside world was forgotten. In between singing I played gently on the piano and we talked of this and that. Jan, in his grubby clothes and white and red armband, with exhaustion and quiet courage etched on his face, was somehow the very essence of a Home Army soldier. He was about 22 or 23, already knew the grim realities of battle, and would be going into action again in a couple of hours' time.

Reluctantly, we drew things to a close. The small knots of people standing and chatting had dispersed by now. It was time for us to get back to our clinic and start getting things ready for the night. Krysta and I started to pick our way across the bricks and debris.

We were just approaching our base when a great bombardment started. 'Mooo-moooooooooo' went the horrible rakietnica, screaming towards us ... we made for the back of the building, which seemed to afford us better protection than the rooms opening on to the street, and we instinctively crouched down close to the floor as the bombardment intensified.

Crash! Boom! Crunch! Our world collapsed. It's impossible to describe the noise of half a wall falling near to you.

'That was a close one!' Words are inadequate when you have just escaped death by a matter of yards. Everything seemed to sway precariously − a great roaring and rumbling noise showed that not far away some building had caught the worst of the explosion. As soon as we dared to move, we made our way to the front of our block. The room there was a complete shambles. Dirt, rubble, dust and broken glass covered everything, and we saw it through a fog of powdered masonry. Coughing and finding it hard to breath, we started to scrabble about to try to salvage what we could of our precious equipment.

'Evacuate! We've got to evacuate!' The order came briskly, telling us to move into a stronger and as yet undamaged block across the street. Fortunately, no one in our clinic or its attendant bedrooms had been killed − apart from cuts and bruises all was well and we could concentrate on looking after the wounded who would start to pour in on us within the next few minutes. We scrambled together what we could, dusting things off, and then hurried outside.

As the dust cleared everywhere, a scene of chaos emerged. We ran to help people who were trying to drag their wounded towards us across the ruins. We had to get the worst cases to the hospital in Mokotowska, while trying to give what first-aid we could to those whom we could help on the spot. We hauled the bleeding and the dying to safety, reassuring the panic-stricken, trying to work quickly. Out of the blur and mess I saw one woman with blood pouring from her, slumped against a wall. I shouted at her to reach out towards me, but she was semi-conscious, losing a lot of blood and unable to move. She was a large middle-aged woman, virtually a dead weight to carry, and I still can't imagine how I achieved it but I got hold of her under her waist and pulled one of her arms round my shoulders and managed to haul her along. I dragged her to Mokotowska Street to the hospital: it was a scene of horrific chaos with patients − babies, soldiers, old people − all with open wounds dumped everywhere and exhausted doctors and orderlies staggering under the workload. The woman's blood was pumping out over me. No one among the grey-faced exhausted staff had a second glance for yet another patient. I half shouted and half sobbed: 'I got her here — now come and help — come and do something', the words choking out in anger and breathlessness, and finally hands reached out from somewhere and the burden was shared.

We worked until late into the night. Once the immediate flow of wounded had received attention, and we had dug out everyone we could from among the ruins, we started the work of salvaging what we could from our clinic to organise things properly at our new base. We searched systematically through the rubble, handing things out to one another, cleaning them off, carrying them across. I was in the middle of doing this when Krysta brought news that the 'peżet' hall had been hit. Jan was dead.

Years later, when we were both middle-aged women, Krysta wrote a little article for a Polish newspaper about Jan and me singing together at the piano, and how I had looked when I learned of his death just a few hours later. At the time, there wasn't even the luxury of finding fifteen minutes alone in which to cry quietly for a Home Army soldier and one short afternoon of music in a half-ruined hall.

NOTES

Chapter 10
1. Many years later I was to meet up with him in London, and we recognised each other at once. Some faces and experiences are written into your memory for ever.
2. Many years after the war, Father Kwiecinski met my young son and showed him the silver container. On one corner was a big dent and Father Kwiecinski demonstrated how this had been made — by a German bullet which had lodged there, thus missing his heart and saving his life.

Chapter Eleven

In the new centre that we established for ourselves on the opposite side of Krucza Street things were a good deal more primitive than they had been in our first post. There was no space to arrange separate accommodation for the in-patients and the 'walking wounded'. We all shared the rooms together, and established ourselves as best we could. It was in the messy and difficult hours of transferring everything that I came to appreciate Wisia's qualities, especially her quite orderliness: with quick movements she went efficiently about her work, sorting things out with undramatic attention to important details.

We soon realised that the massive bombardment which had been unleashed on us was part of a bigger offensive chiefly directed to the Old Town. In the first hours after the attack we were all too busy working to be able to take an interest in the strategic picture, but later news filtered through, and it was grim indeed.

It was evident that the Old Town could not hold out much longer. A pall of smoke hung over it and at night orange flames lit up the sky. Exhausted ourselves, snatching an hour of sleep when we wanted five – or ten – and feverishly working to deal with horrific wounds using inadequate equipment, our hearts went out to the people there, caught in an infinitely worse plight, and with the enemy on the point of breaking through to them.

We heard the details of the battle for the Old Town finally when it fell and some of its survivors found their way to us through the only route open to them – the sewers.

For weeks, we had all been using the cellars of houses,

and the use of underground routes had become normal and familiar to us. In fact along all the main highways the stumbling clamber from cellar to cellar had become the chief means of communication, for messages and the distribution of supplies. But beneath this lay a still more underground route yet: the stifling, stinking, pitch-black tunnels filled with human excrement, which had formed the city's sewage system for nearly a hundred years.

By the time the Old Town fell, there was little left for the soldiers to fight for. The Old Town was in ruins. Any semblance of normal life had vanished. It was simply a maze of rubble and half-destroyed buildings in which grey-uniformed Germans and the indifferently-clad Home Army battled it out yard by yard. We later learned of hand-to-hand fighting within the shells of buildings, and of firing from pew to pew in the ancient churches, where soldiers darted behind pillars and hid out in the remains of side-chapels and odd corners.

Finally, when the Germans broke through, those of our soldiers who were not killed took to the sewers, struggling back to the last sectors of the city still in Polish hands in a timeless pitch-black horror of filth that defies description. Some were lost down there and died in the impenetrable darkness. Others only reached the surface after hours of wandering, collapsing at the feet of their rescuers. In our sector of the city, people waited by the cover of each manhole, listening for the arrival of the soldiers. Everyone would strain to hear the faintest of sounds from far below, and then when the stragglers appeared would haul them up to the surface.

The stench of these brave men and women was terrible. They had had to wade in waist-high human excrement, in which floated rats and the dead bodies of the comrades who had failed to survive the horrifying journey. At a manhole, they had to listen intently, trying to check if the voices they could hear from the surface were Polish or German. Those who had been wandering in the tunnels had no means of knowing what battles had been raging above their heads while they groped in the darkness.

Many had set out on the journey already badly wounded.

Many lost consciousness on the trek because of the fumes and lack of oxygen, and could not be revived.

When the survivors emerged, they dripped raw sewage from their tattered clothes. Exhausted beyond all normal human endurance, they waited patiently whilst we ran hither and thither filling our blue and white enamel buckets with water to wash them down. Our help seemed so inadequate against the enormity of their need. Most were crawling with lice and their wounds were infected: even before entering the sewers they had been unable to wash or receive medical treatment for many days. We used tweezers to pick lice out of the open wounds, and all day fires burned in the courtyard heating bucket after bucket of water for washing them.[1]

We were not able to use gas for cooking or heating water now − the gas connections had been smashed in the bombardment. Over the open fires our boilers and pans were adequate for our needs provided there were enough willing hands to fill and carry them. There was also no electricity, and no water in the pipes.

Meanwhile we were still getting other patients. It was at this stage that I forged an unforgettable bond with a little Jewish boy. His father, Mr L. a pale, frightened young man, came to our makeshift clinic to beg for help, saying that his son was very ill. The family had evidently been in hiding somewhere for a long time, and now like everyone else was caught up in the Rising. Mr L. was young and very nervous. When I went back to where the family was living, I saw at once that the little boy was very seriously ill indeed. He was about five or six years old. There could be no mistaking the symptoms − the high temperature and fever, the particular blotchy red look of the skin, and much else, pointed to just one thing: scarlet fever. The illness had given him an inflammation of the inner ear which was evidently causing him great pain.

'I'll have to get a doctor to confirm this,' I said rather nervously, 'I'll be back'.

When I duly reported the information to my post, Dr Jan's reaction was an angry one. 'Scarlet fever − are you sure? It's an appallingly infectious disease. Have you had it yourself? No? Then you're putting yourself at risk. And now you're asking me to go and bring it back to pass on to our wounded soldiers. I can't do that. What are you thinking about?' When I could get a word in, I pleaded for the little boy. He was only a child. He might die. He was in pain. We couldn't seriously just leave him to his fate.

At first I didn't seem to make much headway.

'We're an army hospital. We've got to sort out our priorities. You can't put our front-line soldiers at risk because of one civilian patient.' But he came in the end, and confirmed my diagnosis, as I had known he would. There wasn't much he could prescribe in the way of drugs because we had none available, but we did have aspirin for the fever, and he outlined the basic treatment I should give the little boy.

From then on I visited the family twice a day to dress the child's ear and to check on his progress. The ear was a delicate job involving the use of strips of fine gauze and some of my precious antiseptic powders dissolved in water, to clean out the pus and messy discharge. The child hovered between life and death and the young parents − neither of them can have been over thirty − watched him every moment. Eventually it was clear that he had passed the crisis. In their gratitude and relief they were still haunted by fear − after spending all of the Occupation in hiding and now emerging under heavy fire with perhaps a prospect of a German breakthrough, terror must have become a normal part of their lives.

Janek was up and about now, back on duty and a great help to us as a source of news, supplies, and information.

Not much of the news was good. We heard about the fate of various friends, or rumours about the Soviet army or airlifts.

Supplies of food, not very abundant at the start of the Rising, were now beginning to run low. The 'peżet' was still doing its best but still the situation deteriorated. Naturally, the priority was to feed our patients − we found that we ourselves could manage on surprisingly little. We were so busy − there wasn't time to dwell on thoughts of food.

It was a tragedy that the Rising had begun before the harvest of the countryside around Warsaw had been gathered in. The momentum of war cannot wait for such things. The potato crop, which would have been such a boon, was still out in the fields.

From somewhere, Janek managed to get hold of some sugar — quite a lot of it, in sugar-lump form. We found that one lump, with a dash of vodka on it, slowly sucked to make it last as long as possible, was surprisingly effective in renewing energy and vitality.

We got ourselves reasonably well organised in these new quarters. Wisia arranged for all the beds that had not been damaged to be carried across, and the patients were settled as comfortably as we could manage, in the cellars and ground floor to give them maximum protection. For our own sleeping arrangements we used an old-fashioned sofa and an armchair — or failing that, the floor. We all swapped around, so that everyone got a chance to get some rest. When we got the chance to sleep, we would remove our belts and shoes — the latter were in a terrible state of repair by now — and fall asleep there and then.

One evening I realised that I had been scratching myself at intervals all day, trying to rid myself of uncomfortable itching, especially on my head. A quick check with Ada and Krysta revealed that they were in the same plight. We took a good look at one another's hair, parting the locks and peering at the roots. Our worst fears were realised: we had got nits and lice. Washing was quite ineffective for getting rid of these pests — you needed proper medication which we didn't have.

We had been trying to keep ourselves as clean as possible. Whenever we got the chance we washed ourselves and our clothing, but we had so little of the latter that regular changes were not possible and we had to go on wearing the same old dirty and smelly garments day after day. Everyone was more or less in the same position — indeed we were luckier than some, as at least we had access to buckets and even to limited amounts of soap.

We realised we would simply have to live with the nits and lice, and the itching was one more penalty of the battlefield. If I had known then that I was not to be free of the wretched things for over a year I don't think I would have been so calm about it.

Another horror that now arrived was dysentery. This was a direct result of the impossibility of keeping things clean. People started to get violent stomach cramps and to pass blood. Dysentery is a horrible disease to try to combat. It is debilitating, highly contagious, and very humiliating for the sufferer. The worst thing for the victims was not having a proper change of clothes. The horrible smell of excrement, the hurried use of buckets in emergencies, the pain and the sense of disgust could not even be relieved by the comfort of a decent bath and the offer of a clean set of underwear. We all coped as best we could, struggling to make use of anything available.

Over and above everything else, however, came the battle itself, raging around us in the streets. Dr Zygmunt's great sense of calm, and his ability to concentrate on the matter in hand, really came into their own now. If there was a bombardment while he was operating he just carried on as if there was nothing to think about except the work in front of him.

We knew that the Germans, having recaptured the Old Town to our north, must inevitably now be drawing daily closer towards us. In fact much later when I got a fuller picture I found they were closing in from the south as well, moving in from Mokotow.

All that we knew was that things were steadily getting more difficult – and that the only thing to do was to keep up our courage and fight on. We couldn't believe we would be abandoned. The baffling silence of the Soviet guns could not last for ever, and they must surely move westward across the Vistula any day now. We heard rumours all the time about their presence.

Water was now the main problem. The taps were running dry, and so we had to rely directly on the city's old wells. These were functioning adequately but the problem was fetching the water. We had to have constant relays of people going out with buckets on such expeditions. Each trip was time-consuming and risky. The wells were across on the other side of Ujazdow Allee, and the journey was horrid.

We took a bucket in each hand and headed off, running

in a crouched position and then darting behind barricades to hide from gunfire, running again, jumping and scrambling over ruins. On arrival we stood in a queue for what seemed ages. Then came the journey back — much harder because we were carrying filled buckets and still faced the risks of snipers and explosives. Ujazdow Allee itself was the hardest part. Jumping and running with a bucket sloshing about is not easy. Every precious drop spilt meant a bit of the journey wasted.

I begged Mr L., in return for the nursing help I was giving his little boy, to take a turn at the water relays as we needed every pair of hands. Poor man, he was so very scared and nervous. He did go once or twice, but he was difficult to persuade on each occasion. He had lived so long in hiding, with the terrible knowledge of what was happening to Jews, that his fear was understandable.

Our bandages had originally been packed in hermetically sealed wrappings, a guarantee of their sterility. We were using them again and again and we needed huge amounts of water for boiling them. We also needed it for sterilising instruments — and of course for washing our patients, their wounds and their clothing. Because we now had no disinfectants at all, we were boiling everything for twenty minutes instead.

A fresh bombardment started while I was assisting Dr Zygmunt at an operation. His calm remained unruffled. Crash! Boom! Crump! A very close one. Everything shook. Something hit me. Bits of the ceiling were falling in.

Dr Zygmunt didn't falter. He just went on with his work, motioning for what he needed. With shaking hands, but in silence, Wisia and I were picking bits of plaster out of the patient. Incredibly, he survived.

We had moved the sickest people down to the cellars — it was a lot safer there. I became friendly with one young man, Tadeusz. All the young soldiers idealised us nurses. They saw us as angels or heroines, and poured out to us all the affection and tenderness they were unable to show to absent wives, girlfriends, mothers or sisters. There was even a song about us — one of the popular songs of the Rising. It was about a girl called Margaret, who had a smart flat in the

Allee of the Roses, and a chic little dog. She wore beautiful clothes and high-heeled shoes, and got a fashionable tan from sitting on the beach by the river. And then she became a nurse when the fighting broke out, and served in the front line — more beautiful than ever, with a lovely smile 'and always as nice as honey'. I think there really was an original Margaret on whom the song was based: at any rate it sang the praises of girls who had been used to comfortable lives and smart clothing, but who were now working under conditions as harsh and squalid as any that could be imagined.

Tadeusz was about 28, a good-looking young man who was probably quite tall, although it was difficult to tell as I only ever saw him lying in bed. We were dealing with some terrible wounds now. Some had been caused by shrapnel, others by debris from falling buildings. There wasn't a single clean wound and the stench that arose from some was nauseating. We did our best to get rid of the lice, but they always seemed to get the better of us, and no matter how thorough we tried to be they would re-appear as if from nowhere, and wander around under the bandages.

The mood among our wounded, especially those from the Old Town, was often bitter and cynical — they covered what they were really feeling with wry jokes.

When there was firing, we all went down to the cellars to be with the patients. 'Don't leave me, Sister — please don't leave me!' The fear of the bed-ridden was that they would be trapped down there. Again and again we had to reassure them that under no circumstances would we run away and leave them — whatever happened we were all in this together.

Food was now very short and all our normal supplies had more or less stopped. We had begun to wonder just what we were going to be able to give the patients. Then some one arrived with an important announcement: a big brewery had been captured in Muranow: it had some grain in its store and volunteers were need to go and get it.

We all knew the journey would be hazardous — Muranow was a good way off — but we'd be going at night and anyway the need was desperate. We could make some sort of porridge for the patients from the grain: the choice was between collecting the grain or starving.

I volunteered to go and we found the biggest bag we could: one that I could wear on my back, leaving my hands free to clamber through the cellars and in and out of the ruined buildings.

It was a mixed group that gathered that night: about twenty of us, all ages right down to a little boy of about nine or ten. We set off, moving swifting and stealthily, dodging and ducking, then waiting, hiding in a safe corner until given the signal to go on. Even apart from the risk of being shot, it was a tricky journey because of the mountains of rubble, sudden steep drops and looming ruins. You could trip and fall very easily.

At the brewery, our sacks and bags were filled to capacity: we all needed to carry as much as we possibly could. There were big shovels which made the task easier. It was coarse, unmilled grain, still with its husks on. It had originally been stored in the warehouse because it was waiting to be made into beer. We could make a rough sort of 'kasza' with it. We helped each other to fill every bag and then gathered for the journey back.

This was much tougher going. You couldn't run or jump, and the heaviness of our loads slowed us down and made us feel very vulnerable. The worst moment was when some one noticed that the little boy's sack had a hole in it, and that he had already lost a good quantity of the precious grain we had all been risking so much to get. I shall never forget the stricken look on his little face, and his stalwart attempts not to cry. He had been told to behave like a soldier, like a worthy son of Poland, and he was doing his very best, but it's not easy when you are nine years old and bitterly distressed and feel that you have let everyone down ... 'Here, let me help' 'Let's tie a good big knot, like this ...' Everyone helped to repair the damage, and we stumbled on back.

We boiled up the grain and made what everyone came to call 'kasza pluj' or 'spit-porridge' because you had to chew it carefully and then spit out the hard dry husks after each mouthful. It made the mouth and gums very sore – and was particularly unsuitable for very sick people – but it was all we had so there was no use complaining about it.

The days, and more particularly the nights, were now

getting colder. It was September. Still no move from the Soviet army and the airlifts from the Western allies seemed to have come to a complete halt.

In our small unit we were determined to fight on to the end. The mood among the civilian population had inevitably shifted from that heady optimism and self-sacrifice shown in the first fortnight to a certain grim endurance. There had been so many deaths, and people had been forced to endure so much. What was amazing was that one heard no complaints or recriminations. With no food, and only limited water, it was hard to see what hope we could hold out.

We had grown used to a sense of complete exhaustion: if we slept for a couple of hours some one would almost invariably wake us with some new arrivals. There were always more wounded from the latest round of firing and fighting: more water needed, attempts to soothe and reassure, a scramble for bandages and equipment — 'Don't worry, it's all right. This is a clinic . . . we'll look after you.' Eyes dazed with pain, wounds filthy — some horrific — voices pleading for help.

Now the Germans began a massive, systematic bombardment. Every day, several times a day, always at roughly the same hour, street by street, the missiles ruthlessly closed in on us. You felt them coming nearer and nearer with each round of firing, and you knew that your turn must come soon.

We were practically all living in the cellars now.

'It's all right — I won't leave you. Of course I won't leave you.' We practically had to swear it on the Bible to reassure these boys, down here in the bowels of the earth with a great booming and shuddering overhead. When the mooing sound started, you could count one, two, three . . . and on the count of six the crash would come.

Tadeusz was holding my hand. 'Here, Sister Irena, I want you to have this.' He fumbled under his pillow and brought out a fountain pen — a really nice one, a Waterman of English make. 'It's for you — I want you to keep it for always. It belonged to my brother . . . and now I want to give it to you.'

I knew Tadeusz' brother had been killed a couple of weeks

before. I looked into his eyes and knew that he was giving
me his most precious possession. I couldn't say anything.
He pressed the pen into my hand. I still have it.

The booming and crashing above was getting louder and
his grip tightened. I held on to him, this helpless boy trapped
in bed in the darkness of an underground cellar. Close to
each other, trying to find words of reassurance, we were
there under the ruins of our city. We were young Poles,
lice-ridden, hungry and frightened, but so far undefeated.

NOTES

Chapter 11

1. Mrs Wanda Sarnecka, now living in London, who was a liaison
    girl from the Old Town recalls: 'We knew when we had reached
    the Polish-occupied parts of the city because there, helping to
    haul us to the surface, were normal-looking people, girls with
    clean faces and decent clothes and even lipstick. It was a sight
    we hadn't seen for weeks — something belonging to a different
    world. We could hardly believe it. We had been making our
    way through areas of the city where the battle lines were
    unclear and where every house might be in enemy hands. In the
    Old Town we had been bombarded systematically every half
    hour until virtually every building was destroyed — and the
    Germans were also using the most hated weapon of all, the
    flame-thrower which burned everything in its path ... You
    will not meet many survivors from the Old Town who are able
    to talk about it very easily. For us, reaching another part of
    the city that was still Polish-held meant discovering Poland
    again. This was what it was all about, what we were fighting
    for.'

Chapter Twelve

It was when the silence fell that we knew something had happened. Suddenly the bombardment, explosions, and shooting stopped. The silence was a horrible one, there was no peace in it, just a sort of ache — a dry tension. It was momentarily like the silence in Autumn 1939 when the city fell to the Germans after holding out following the invasion. It was eerie.

Rumours began to spread and then we were told officially: General Bor had gone with a delegation to the Germans to parley with them.

Among our team — Wisia, Krysta, Ada, Janek and me — the feeling was that we would hold out to the end, or until we died. Death had long since lost its fear. Many of our friends had died.

Years later, after the war, I saw a film about the battle for Paris. So much had faint echoes of our experience: the years of occupation, the sufferings endured, the secret underground army loyal to an exiled government in London. Yet in all essentials everything was so terribly different: the Parisians had help marching towards them all the way, a glorious day of liberation when troops finally reached the city, that marvellous march down the Champs Elysées, girls blowing kisses and tossing flowers on to the tanks .... I couldn't bear to watch the end part of the film. For us in Warsaw, the battle was so tragically uneven. The help never came — we were abandoned to our fate. And yet our spirit was every bit as tough as that of the Parisians — indeed, probably tougher, since we had endured a far more savage form of German occupation, and for longer.

'Maybe there'll be some planes – maybe even now. Perhaps it's taken all this while to hammer out some agreement. Perhaps the Russians ....' We sat in the cellars trying to give our patients what relief we could with whatever we had left. Even a drink of water was now a luxury.

There was no question of running for shelter: these walls were our last defence. If they held up, well and good – we'd survive another day. If not, we'd simply be among the others who had already died.

We were not really surprised when an order came about the evacuation of civilians. Our AK command announced that an agreement had been reached about this with the Germans. We heard the news knowing that the battle was reaching its last stages. The people of Warsaw were now presented with a grim set of alternatives – they could leave, taking with them only what they could carry, or they could stay and probably die with the remnants of the AK in the last desperate round of the battle.

People leaving the city were not given any assurances about where they would be allowed to settle, or whether they would be allowed to return. The only commitment from the Germans was to a cease-fire while the actual evacuation took place, and safe conduct to towns and villages outside the city.

They would all be heading off to an unknown future, leaving behind them what remained of their homes, furniture, family goods, and precious oddments that had survived the fighting. They would leave the graves of many they loved, and many would also leave members of their families behind – everyone who was serving in the AK would stay on, to fight to the bitter end.

The order about the departure of civilians thus caused a great deal of heart-searching and anguish. Two dates were set on which they could go. They were not given very long in which to make up their minds. The amnesty during which they could leave was to be of very specific duration.

The L. family, whose little boy I had nursed, were among those who elected to go. Still terrified – indeed more so, as they were placing themselves directly at the mercy of the

Nazis — they came to say good-bye. Mr L. pressed into my hand a ring.

'This if for you, for saving the life of our little boy'. They had been a well-to-do family and had various bits of gold and jewellery with them. Now they walked off to join the columns of people trudging out of the city. Families carried bags and bundles — everyone was weak and hungry and few could manage to drag along very much. Children trailed along, and babies were carried in arms. Our Warsaw, with its families and its schools, its cafés, shops, concerts, museums, industry and commerce, was being scattered to the winds.

Among us, the AK remnants, the feeling was now that we should fight on until either death or the arrival of Allied help spelt the end. Our lives seemed to have no purpose apart from this — to have struggled on against such terrible odds for so long seemed pointless if in the end there was to be a capitulation. And hope about Allied support took a long while to die. At this stage, deep in our hearts we still could not bring ourselves to accept that the nations which had gone to war over us were really going to abandon us completely now the crunch had come.

Meanwhile we still had work to do. We were trying to look after our patients as best we could. Janek was busy trying to collect together anything that might be useful to us for whatever lay ahead. He had got for me a pair of German boots — a real boon since my shoes had by now completely disintegrated. They weren't the knee-high jackboots the Germans often wore but a shorter variety. They were sturdy and in good condition. 'We've got to look ahead to the cold weather and the winter' said Janek grimly. He also acquired from somewhere a jacket for me — a good one with pockets and a collar. I already had an army sidecap on which I wore a white and red Home Army ribbon.

We talked about the terms that General Bor might now be negotiating with the Germans. While the Soviets could watch, their guns silent, from the other side of the Vistula, the last days of Warsaw's bitter drama were played out.

We nurses discussed together what we should do in the event of our being marched away as prisoners of war. There were now six of us in the team. We agreed that three would go with the 'walking wounded' into prison camps or wherever we were sent. The other three would remain with those too ill to move. We were not optimistic about the plight of these. The last few weeks had taught us something of how the Germans treated Polish wounded. The stories about them just opening up the door of a cellar and throwing in grenades were not fabrications. Any promise on their part that the wounded would be taken to hospital could not be believed until it was actually carried out.

When the decision was made, I was among those detailed to go into imprisonment with those who were able to walk. Wisia would remain with the more seriously wounded patients. Our two doctors also split their services – Dr Jan to go to the camps and Dr Zygmunt to remain behind. We now learned that in the grim negotiations that were taking place between General Bor and the German commanders, a major issue was our status. He was asking for the recognition of our rights as prisoners-of-war. We were proper combatant soldiers and not civilians, and entitled to protection under the Geneva Convention, which Germany had signed before the war. This was a vital point which he did win.

And now the end came. Exhausted, out of every possible scrap of food and ammunition, we had to hear the command that we cease active resistance to the Germans, and that we accept the inevitable. We gathered in groups and the order was formally given to us. This was done in a military way: we all kept our dignity and the final statement from our commander was addressed to us as soldiers, the sorrow too evident in every phrase and echoed in every listening heart. We stood straight at attention. Our battle to free Warsaw had lasted two months.

Tadeusz was one of those too ill to walk. The goodbyes were very, very difficult. It was very hard indeed to convince ourselves that out of all this anguish, courage and sorrow could come any good at all. We squeezed hands and could not say very much.

It is difficult to express just what capitulation meant to us. Of course we recognised the impossibility of our position – but to have this as the end of five years of struggle seemed so heartbreaking. The determination to win, even against hopeless odds, had not seemed crazy — and yet as we looked around, the desolated ruins, the dead bodies and the ill and wounded told their own story.

The final hours had a starkness about them that makes every detail unforgettable.

The most dramatic and tragic part of our capitulation was the surrender of our arms. The guns and other weapons gathered at so much cost and sacrifice now had to be handed over to our enemies as the final climax of our defeat. There were various collecting points and the task was carried out with military discipline. It was the final act before we were marched off as prisoners of war.

We were determined to leave as soldiers. Formed up in ranks, wearing our torn and battleworn clothing, we tried to square our shoulders and hold our heads up. This wasn't easy, as many people were collapsing from lack of food and water. I stood with Ada and Krysta, with whom I had similarly lined up when we were marched as hostages in front of the tanks.

The Germans were not content with simply marching us away to imprisonment. They seemed determined to force on us a full sight of our ruined city first. When we assembled at our rallying-points they started us on a long trudge that took us round every part of what had been our battlefield. As we had all been confined to our own immediate areas of the fighting, we had not known the full scope of the devastation. Not a building still stood intact: every loved landmark had gone or been reduced to a hideous stump or pathetic ruin. The cathedral, the various churches, the great apartment blocks, all the shops and offices ... most streets and squares were just completely unrecognisable. No longer sheltering teams of exhausted fighters protecting tiny pockets of Polish life, the ruins seemed to have no purpose any more. In the thick dust the stench of death, with which we had been living for so long, rose up from many of them.

In this city we had buried so many friends and comrades-in-arms. Here there were so many lost hopes and vanished dreams.

The forced march was very slow. We were halted several times and were made to wait for long periods. No water was

given to us, and we were not given permission to sit down.
At one point our unit passed a group of men in German
uniform. We recognised them as Hungarians — they were
among various units of different nationalities fighting under
German command against us in those last days in Warsaw.
We stiffened up and tried to make an extra effort to march
as soldiers.

We attempted a song, but with dry throats and exhausted
bodies the music didn't come easily. Many people had collapsed and were having to be helped along anyway: others
slumped by the wayside and we had to try to revive them
and improvise ways of carrying them between us. These were
people who should have been left as bedridden wounded but
who were desperate to come with us as they feared their fate
at the hands of the Germans if they were left behind.

At one halt, in front of one of Warsaw's big hospitals,
a group of doctors and staff was standing watching. A
face stood out among them — the principal of the Warsaw
School of Nursing. She recognised me and we managed a
few moments of talk, swapping news. 'How was it for you?'
'What have these last few days been like in your area?' Two
years before she had been handing my diploma to me, in an
atmosphere of clean dresses and congratulations and posies
of flowers.

I also briefly saw my aunt — mother of my cousin Valery
who had been wounded alongside Janek. I gave her my latest
news of him, as he and Janek had left the previous day (we
were being marched out on two consecutive days, October
5th and 6th).

These chance meetings with these two women were to be
my last real links with the Warsaw in which I had grown up,
the city which I loved and which had been my home.

Eventually we reached what had once been a railway
station at Ozarow, some way out of Warsaw. The whole
railway network was of course no longer functioning in any
normal way, but the lines were there and the trains would
roll into the Reich. We had no idea where we would be taken.
We were divided by sexes, ready for the prison-camps, and
kept waiting a long time. The first group of AK prisoners —
those who had left Warsaw the previous day — were already

here, in a big disused factory hall, and so after some hunting I found Janek and Valery again. It was a brief and poignant meeting, because the time for further goodbyes came only too quickly. A train arrived, consisting of a long line of cattle trucks.

The trucks had no benches or seats. We were ordered in, and we sat or stood on the bare wooden boards with our little bundles. We nurses were anxiously holding on to our bags of dressings and bandages because we hoped that whenever the train stopped we might be able to look after our patients who were officially in our charge but had been herded into another truck as we were split into groups of males and females.

As we started to roll away from devastated Warsaw, we set to work to cope with the first immediate problem: the lack of a bucket for use as a lavatory. Someone had a penknife and we chipped away at the floorboards in one corner of the trucks to make a hole. 'Hurry — oh, hurry — I can't hold it!' Girls were clutching their stomachs, feeling degraded and distraught. The hole provided them with relief but of course no privacy or hygiene. Pretty soon the stench in the airless truck became appalling.

We had no idea of our exact destination, but we knew we were heading west — into Germany. By clambering up on top of one another, we could peer briefly through the tiny grating up by the roof, and try to catch a glimpse of any town or landmark that we might be passing.

We all wrote notes on tiny scraps of paper, giving our names, former addresses, and any information we could, telling what had happened in Warsaw, begging anyone who found the note to pass on news to our families. 'Quick — we're passing what looks like a town —' No one recognised the place, but the knowledge that we were near ordinary people somehow gave us a sense of encouragement. The notes were hurriedly finished and slipped through the grille.[1]

Lice and nits assisted in making the journey a time of maximum discomfort. Not one of us was free of them, and without water we could not even wash. Anxiety and fear — about our families, and everything we had left behind in Warsaw and were now about to face in Germany — were the dominant feelings.

Once or twice the trucks ground to a halt and the guards came banging on the doors shouting 'Raus! Raus!' We were told we could relieve ourselves along by the railway line. The guards stood over us while we did so, guns at the ready in case we tried to escape. Some girls, already ill, found it impossible to perform their natural functions with men staring at them. The dysentery sufferers had to relieve themselves constantly and had lost embarrassment, but others began to get swollen stomachs from an inability to use either the hole in the truck or the open fields.

For those of us who were nurses, the brief stop allowed a quick visit to the wounded. I ran up to the men's trucks further down the line, and changed people's dressings and gave advice as swiftly as I could. My thoughts flew briefly to Wisia, back in Warsaw with the other patients, and I wondered how she was getting on.

The trucks were high and hard to reach and there was a lot of scrambling and jumping. The guards shouted 'Schnell!' at us all the time to make us hurry.

In all, the journey took about a week, with many long stops when we remained sealed in the trucks.

After a time, the days and nights merged into one another.

We knew, however, when we reached the border. A girl looking out through the grill reported what she could see, and told us we had reached the frontier. As the train rolled across, we started to sing one of our national songs – and we heard it going from truck to truck with its poignant chorus 'We will never leave our country ... we will never leave our country ... '

NOTES

Chapter 12

1. I discovered much later – after the war – that a cousin of mine had been given my note. She lived in the town through which we had passed, and the note was passed to her by someone who had picked it up. It seems likely that people rushed to the train, knowing it came from Warsaw, and were on the look-out for any messages.

An impression of how the scene looked from outside the train is given by Leokadia Jaromirska, recalling Ozorow Station, Poland, in the Autumn of 1944, in *Avenue of the Righteous*, published in 1980: 'A train passed through loaded with prisoners from the uprising. Warsaw had surrendered. Seeing those military caps with the Polish eagle, we cried. They threw out messages on scraps of paper in the hope that they might eventually reach their families. These men were being taken to a concentration camp in Germany. As the train pulled slowly through the station, they sang the Polish national anthem.'

Chapter Thirteen

The train came to its final, jolting halt. This was Germany. The guards came shouting 'Raus! Raus!' and we were ordered out of the trucks and marched off.

We were very pleased indeed when we discovered we were going to have a shower – even though this meant stripping completely under the gaze of the guards. All our clothing was taken away – we were told it was going to be disinfected – and we were marched through to a large room with shower-heads protruding from the ceiling. The water emerged either freezing cold or scaldingly hot, and in intermittent bursts. It felt so good to have even a semblance of cleanliness. Nothing could be done about the nits in our hair – washing with water alone was wholly ineffective at getting rid of them. Most of us just had to live with this misery until the end of the war.

It was this shower that confirmed our status as prisoners of war. For too many others, the destination was a different sort of camp and the gas chambers. We now knew we must be protected by having military status, the one concession wrung from the victors in Warsaw.

Still naked, we were made to line up in two columns and taken to another room where we were kept waiting. Then a door opened at the other end and in marched our men, also naked. The moment they saw us they turned their backs to spare us all humiliation – a gesture of decency that was a reminder of civilised values.

Long queues formed in front of the primitive wooden sheds that housed the lavatories. Many girls were now acutely suffering with swollen and distended stomachs from being unable to relieve themselves on the long journey – others still suffered from untreated dysentery.

Finally, we were given our clothes back, and put on another transport that was to take us to a prison-camp. It was a *stalag*, a camp for all ranks, and was at Sandbostel between Bremen and Hamburg. A large contingent of Polish prisoners was already there, mostly people who had been captured back in '39. Hearing of our arrival, they had done their best to prepare for us, laying down straw for us to sleep on.

Women were allocated to two barracks in different parts of the camp. We were completely separated from the Polish men and I was no longer able to nurse them. After a short spell in one barracks I was transferred to the other, where my nursing skills were needed as a number of the women were seriously ill. A new chapter was beginning.

The camp had been established on very damp land – the huts were built on stilts on the marshes. We had to sleep on wood shavings and these soaked up moisture with horrible ease, so that we shivered at night and woke each morning damp and cold and aching in every limb. The irony was that although everything was soaking wet we were always thirsty and desperately short of water for our own basic needs. Each morning we were issued with our ration for the day – a tiny bowlful. The bowls being the size of pudding-basins. What were we to do with this minute quantity? Drink it? Wash tiny bits of ourselves in it? Or wash our clothes? The choice was an agonising one as we so wanted to get ourselves a little bit clean. Everyone just tried to do the best they could.

With so many prisoners gathered together at the camp, there was a chance to exchange news and information. All of us had been involved in the battle in different parts of Warsaw, and had not had a chance to see the wider picture. Now, gradually, we each began to piece it all together. Tragically, every fresh bit of information simply meant the discovery of more friends who had been killed. I leaned about various colleagues from the Warsaw School of Nursing, and other friends of the early days of the Occupation, who had been caught up in the fighting in different sectors of the city and who I would never see again.

Krysztof Kamil Baczynski's death was the hardest news to bear. When I heard about it my thoughts flew back to the days when I had been nursing him two years earlier, with his bad asthma following his imprisonment in Auschwitz. His fame as a poet had spread, and his words spoke for us all as he wrote about Poland, our faith, war, peace, and our future hopes. Now I heard the details of his death. He had, of course, been an active AK soldier. At the start of the Rising, he had been unable to reach his own unit — many others were also caught in this position, especially with last-minute delays and changes of plan. He did what others did — simply joined the nearest unit to fight with them instead. Then he was shot by a German sniper while out on a patrol. What completed the tragedy was that his wife was killed at about the same time while active with her own unit in another part of the city.

I mourned for this brave and talented man, whose poetry was so beautiful and who had captured the spirit of what we had all been fighting for.

My status as a nurse with an official diploma was formally recognised by the Germans and in this I was different from Ada and Krista who had only been AK first-aid auxiliaries trained by me. They did not have the knowledge or skills for working with the camp's long-term sick people.

Of course I had no nurse's uniform to proclaim my status — only my own worn out clothes. The worst thing was not having a proper change of underwear. But on mine I still had the medal depicting Christ's Mother pinned, close to my heart.

Girls found the lack of a change of clothes, and the inadequate water for washing them, particularly distressing during their periods. At these times, the difficulties became acute. Every scrap of material was pressed into service, and some attempt was made to wash and dry things in ingenious ways. The problem was partially resolved in a curious way — many girls found that their periods stopped while they were in the prison camp. It may have been stress, or simply the poor diet with its lack of vitamins.

Many of the prisoners in another sector of the camp were French, and among them were a couple of specialist French doctors who were able to treat the many ear, nose, and throat problems among us. Ear infections were particularly common because of the damage done by the terrifically noisy bombardment at close range in those last days in Warsaw.

I formed a choir, or rather two of them — one to sing for our religious services and the other concentrating on Polish folk songs and popular music. One day a Polish priest, a prisoner from the men's camp, was allowed to come to see us. This gave people an opportunity to make their confession. He also celebrated a Mass with us. That morning meant a lot to us.

If you did nothing in camp you lost your sense of personality and became like a zombie: we had many girls who were on the brink of this or who had toppled over into complete mental and spiritual breakdown. The slow and bitter struggle in Warsaw, the deaths of parents, friends, lovers, brothers, the starvation, filth and wounds, had been followed by the prison transits, lice and freezing cold with no news from home — or any knowledge that a semblance of home still existed.

The breakdown could take different forms. Some girls just refused to participate in any activities and withdrew to their own silence and inner pain — a form of deep, suppressed hysteria. In others there were curious physical manifestations. One girl could not walk. She had no problem that we could discover in her legs or spine — she wasn't technically paralysed. Her legs just refused to carry her any more. The camp authorities eventually provided a wheelchair and we were able to take her about in it. Some girls simply refused to get up from their bunks and would have sunk into complete inertia if we had not taken firm action. At the beginning of November we had a good reason to make a special effort. We wanted to mark our Polish Independence Day on 11th November. We organised a concert which was a pageant of historical songs, telling the story of Poland's struggle for freedom spanning almost two centuries.

Hunger was an ever-nagging, ever-present reality. We were given a sort of watery soup with three or sometimes four tiny pieces of chopped turnip in it. With this came a ration of bread or potatoes for the day. It seemed very little − but later on as Germany was steadily invaded on all fronts we were to get even less. In these early days in the camp some girls even scraped the skins off their potatoes and threw them aside − although I must add that these peelings weren't actually wasted, as they promptly got eaten by the rest of us! Sometimes the potatoes were completely rotten and almost impossible to eat at all − black and slimy, they disintegrated at a touch.

Some of us were not to be in this camp for very long. It was announced that, in accordance with our prisoner-of-war status, we were to be divided according to ranks. The officers were to go to an *Oflag*, a special camp for those of commissioned status.

We held a discussion and agreed that it was vital that as many as possible of the younger girls came with us, in order that we would look after them and even perhaps offer them some sort of schooling. As officers we felt a responsibility for the girls − many of them not yet out of their teens. There were several of us who could teach different things and so between us we could offer quite a variety of subjects. We also wanted to make sure that the girls got the best possible treatment and care during the period of their imprisonment. They were more vulnerable than the rest of us and we all had fears for the coarsening effect of prison-camp life on them, and shared their frustration at the wasted months and years that should have been devoted to education.

In order to do this, we told the Germans that our officer status entitled us to have girls to look after our needs as orderlies − and, choosing the youngest girls, we were able to take a group to the new camp which would form the nucleus of a Polish school there in the heart of Germany.

It was now getting bitterly cold. It was the beginning of what we all hoped and prayed would be the final winter of the war. We were all desperate to know what was going on back in our native Poland. None of us had heard from parents or families: we did not know whether they were alive or dead, whether the ruins of Warsaw still sheltered some of them or they had all gone to camps and prisons or out to the surrounding countryside. Anxiety gnawed at us all the time: it made some girls ill, driven out of their minds and unable to cope.

The new camp, which we reached after another train journey and a march, was in some respects much better than the old. It had a proper water supply: we could sometimes wash ourselves and our scraps of clothing, although getting the latter dry was a big problem.

We were determined to organise ourselves properly. As in the old camp, we held morning and evening prayers. These are an old tradition in Polish life and in the Polish armed forces. We would say the Our Father together and sing the beautiful hymn which has the same tune for morning and evening, with appropriate words for each. 'When the morning starts ...', the young voices would carol into the freezing air, and beginning the day like this offered new hope and courage to us all, even to those who perhaps were not full believers. And in the evening the same prayer would again be raised, offering to God all that we had done during the day and begging for protection during the night. These times of prayer and praise were a real refreshment giving a special strength that comes from opening yourself to God's presence and getting a sense of His nearness. I don't know what the guards thought.

The nights were bitterly cold. The bunks here were in three tiers, and around the top one the wind howled and screamed, the thin hut walls providing no protection. Sometimes when bundling myself into every scrap of clothing that I had, and trying vainly to arrange things in such a way that every inch of material was used to its fullest extent, I would remember with a wry smile the days when going to bed had actually meant taking everything off, bathing, and slipping into a nightdress.

The administrative staff at this camp – in charge of the kitchens the showers, the stoves and so on – were Italians, interned because of their opposition to Mussolini.

The highest-ranking AK officer among us became our official leader in all liaison with the Germans and a girl who spoke German helped out with translation difficulties. We had a strict sense of military discipline and were conscious of representing our country and showing what it meant to be Polish.

The camp was, of course, miles from any city or town and to reach it we had marched through what seemed miles and miles of open countryside. It was heavily guarded and there was no escape. Where could we go even if we did make it into the open? We had no news about where all the different armies were now placed across the map — we assumed that the various fronts were closing in on Germany and that allies were getting closer to us every day, but we had no access to reliable information.

Our prisoner-of-war status was proclaimed by the numbered metal tags that we carried about with us. These were of the standard sort issued throughout Germany and were designed to be broken in half if you died, with one half returned to your family and the other half buried with your body. I kept this tag for years after the war was over; for a long while it lived, for no particular reason, in my workbasket among the needles and spools of thread, an object of interest to my children and grandchildren.

I was still wearing the jacket that Janek had found for me during the last days of the fighting in Warsaw: its deep pockets were useful for my few possessions. I also still had the side-cap, which helped to keep my head warm.

We soon got a school organised: the younger girls could attend classes in a variety of subjects including history and different languages. I was asked to teach religion: it gave us all an opportunity of sharing something of what the Christian message could mean in our lives.

We were also allowed to make contact with our families once a month: forms were distributed which we could fill in to be posted off to them. None of us received any replies. The war front changed daily and we guessed that all of Poland must by now be well behind the Soviet lines. Years later I found out that members of my family had in fact posted parcels to me giving my name and rank and prisoner status as an address, but none of these ever reached me. They had saved up scraps to send me what they could — dried bread and a bit of fat — but it was all lost in the cross-cross of battle lines slicing Europe.

One day we saw a massive formation of American 'planes overhead and we knew that as we were between Bremen and Hamburg they were heading for one of them to bombard it; we cheered and cheered and felt that at last our liberation was on the way. The raids came with increasing frequency. However the end still did not come.

Christmas arrived and the choir's efforts bore fruit. We had been practising for days, and on Christmas Eve we went from barrack to barrack, pouring our hearts out into our Christmas carols and finding that the words had a real meaning, often perhaps overlooked in happier times. That God shared our humanity − came to earth to be one of us − gave us a message about human dignity that many had forgotten. No Christmas in my life has brought Him as close as that one.

It was around Christmas that we got an issue of Red Cross parcels. There were not enough to go round, so we split each one between four girls: it meant a tiny taste of extra food. In fact some girls decided to enjoy their small ration all at once and got sick as a result!

As the New Year began I was given news of another move. Several women prisoners needed hospital treatment. I was to go with them and work in a prisoner-of-war hospital. I would later discover I was to be the only nurse there, caring for assorted wounded prisoners from different nationalities, in co-operation with Italian doctors.

I collected together my various bits and pieces − including the notes I had made during the Rising, forming a rough diary, which I had brought from Warsaw and was cherishing as a record to show one day what we had all endured and tried to achieve − and made ready to go.

Chapter Fourteen

The hospital was in Nordhausen, in the south of Germany. It was an ordinary house which had been transformed for war use. It was not very large but had a substantial garden. As a hospital, it was fairly primitive, very much a make-do sort of affair. We arrived there after another long train journey, with me in charge of the group of sick women from the camp.

It felt strange to be in an ordinary town instead of in a camp with guard towers and barbed wire. Naturally, we saw nothing of the town itself as we were heavily guarded and not allowed to leave the hospital − but we sensed its presence. From the window I saw only grey skies and the snow falling on the wintry ground.

As the sole nurse, I had my own tiny room. It was not much bigger than a cupboard − but it gave me privacy which I greatly cherished. The hospital had a proper water supply − another joy. Food, of course, continued to be the big problem. Rations had been cut again and we were now down to two wafer-thin slices of bread and two cups of watery 'soup' a day.

This was the final winter of the war and everyone knew it. As spring faintly beckoned, a Polish soldier was among the wounded brought to us. He had very severe head injuries of which he died before we could find out anything about him. Had he been fighting with the Allied armies? Or was he in fact one of the Poles from our western provinces who had been conscripted into the German Wehrmacht? In any event, knowing that he was a fellow countryman all the Poles in the hospital wanted him to have a proper funeral. With an Italian priest prisoner − our hospital chaplain − officiating, this was achieved. The Germans laid on extra guards to make sure that none of us escaped during the service which took place in a local cemetery.

For us, as for all other prisoners-of-war, this was a time of intense, poignant waiting. We knew the Allies could not be so very far away. Our hopes were pinned on the Americans and the British, fighting their way up from the west, and we speculated on how long they would take to reach us. We tried not to think about the wider implications of the movement of the victorious armies across Europe − about the Russians now in our Warsaw trampling over the graves of our dead and claiming rule over whoever remained alive. It was just a question of waiting, surviving, and hoping.

The hospital included many TB patients from among our Polish soldiers. There were two Italian doctors, the Italian priest, and some Italian orderlies − I spoke to them in French which both doctors spoke well. Between us we did the best we could to offer decent medical care within the constraints imposed on us.

On Easter Monday the waiting suddenly came to an abrupt end and the war suddenly exploded around us. With no warning of any kind − no air-raid siren, no shouts − a shattering bombardment broke above our heads and around our ears: the Americans were bombing the town and we were in the heart of the battleground.

In a great scramble we tore about fetching things, hurrying to get the patients into the cellars. There were two of these, one for us prisoners and one for the Germans. We hoped that the patients would be at least marginally safer down below. Few could walk by themselves, and we had to manoeuvre with the stretchers. The roar overhead and around us reached pandemonium as we got the last ones down the steps. There was just time for a desperate scrambling check to make sure no one was left behind, and then I joined the packed crowd down in the cellar. There was not much time to rescue any personal belongings: the priority was to save the patients, and to grab essential supplies of medical equipment and rations.

From the ajoining cellar, where our guards and their families were, we could hear the German voices. Among us there was silence. But it was not a dignified calm. The atmosphere was fraught and sickeningly tense. Everyone was terrified. For the second time in my life I was certain I was about to die. As in the moments of terror as a hostage before the German tanks, I tried to pray. My brain tried to pound out the words. Thick dust and chunks of grit scattered down from the walls as a bomb hit a nearby building. Would we be next? The din overhead was terrific. You could hardly hear yourself think. Thank God, the ceiling held, although it felt as though the whole building itself was rocking.

We had one guard in the room with us, an old soldier, clearly a veteran of the First World War who did not enjoy his role. Like us he was silent, tense and terrified.

The cellar was very old, like the rest of the house. It was not completely underground: a semi-circular window gave access via a recess into the garden. The floor-space was fairly large. patients were propped up against walls or lying on stretchers on the floor. There was not much I could do for them while the bombardment lasted.

After what seemed an eternity of noise and terror, the pounding stopped. Now all was roaring, crackling, and shrieking. The dust began to settle. I got up and blundered my way in the semi-darkness to the door.

More dust and smoke and cascading bits of grit and dirt greeted me as I opened it. The cellar stairs rose up steeply and I walked up them. But there was nothing beyond − only a clear vista of the stars! The house above us had simply ceased to exist. There was no route out this way. The stairs ended in mid-air, against the broken jagged masonry. At any moment more collapse could be expected. Even as we stood there a great roaring and crashing met our ears as the remnants of some of the walls came tumbling down and collapsing in on one another.

'The window!' some one shouted, and we hurried to the cellar's curved semi-circular ventilation point which gave indirect access to the outside world. We worked to pull away the bits of broken glass and rubble, and then started to pass the patients through. It was a long, hot, frightening struggle. Immersed in it, we no longer thought of ourselves as prisoners − only as people desperate to escape from a dangerous building. As I scrambled up and over the heaps of rubble, dragging stretchers into what was until a few hours before the garden, I saw flames leaping into the air in the surrounding streets. Where could we go? Where was there to run to?

A rag-tag band, we struggled out across the grounds of the house. We were all trying to carry what we could, and help one another. The thought leapt starkly into my mind that such small possessions as I had managed to take with me from Warsaw, spare scraps of clothing and the brief diary notes made during the Rising, were now gone for ever.

However, we had more pressing problems. The first street we approached was ablaze, as was the next. A tumbling apartment block crashed inwards with a great roar. We felt trapped in the blazing town, our only thought to find some escape route and head for open country.

Somehow, without quite realising how we had done it, we found ourselves on the edge of the town, with the mountains in the distance ahead of us. At this point our solitary guard, the elderly soldier, left us. 'Deutchland kaput' he said with an air of weary finality 'You go down there, off to the woods. I am going home.' He turned away, and that was the last we saw of him, or of any German soldiers. We were now, in essence, free − but would we survive?

The woods to which he had pointed were some way off but they seemed to offer us some degree of shelter, so we went there ...

And so we lived out the last days of a six-year war, in the last remnant of the Reich, waiting for our liberation, trying to wash in the stream, eating such odd scraps of food as the Italians had managed to bring along, caring for the sick as best we could.

We had to dive for cover from the American planes which were now machine-gunning the woods after air-raids: they were shooting at anything that seemed alive and of course had no idea that we were not Germans but escaped prisoners-of-war from a hospital.

We stuck together, talking and trying to boost each other's morale. I didn't have a comb, a toothbrush, any spare bit of clothing. I finished the war possessing just the grubby worn garments in which I stood, a metal prisoner's tag stating my identity, and a medal of Mary holding Christ in her arms, pinned inside my clothes.

It was a strange vigil. We were entirely ignorant of what battles might be happening to the east and west of us; we simply concentrated on staying alive, and protecting ourselves at night against the cold. I remember the Italians had managed to create some sort of big tent with whatever they had brought out of the cellar − rationing out scraps of food and waiting daily, hourly, for the Americans.

It was late afternoon, almost evening, when they came. I cannot remember how many days it was that we had been in the woods by this time. I just remember the April night beginning to creep up on us, chilly and dark, we hardly believed our own ears when we first heard the sound of voices, straggly at first and then growing louder. We ran from whatever we were doing − and then the American Army, in the shape of a bunch of sturdy helmeted soldiers being there and everyone jabbering, trying to talk to them.

None of us could communicate with them properly as there were no real English speakers amongst us. None of the Americans spoke any Italian, French, or Polish. One of the patients − a Polish girl from my group − had just a few English words and she did her best. We understood only a couple of basic things about the Americans − that they were in a hurry, pointing and saying 'Berlin' and anxious to get there without delay, before the Russians − and that they were very angry, ready to kill any German they met. Later we were to discover the cause of this anger: they had liberated the concentration camps and had seen the horror of them.

Soon more soldiers arrived. These included a chaplain. Our chaplain, the Italian priest, identified himself and the two men hesitantly began to speak to one another in the sole language they had in common − Latin, the ancient language of the Church. Looking back, it was somehow symbolic − these two men in a forest clearing in the remnants of what was once Christendom, communicating vital news in the tongue that was once common to all civilised men. That was how we got the wider picture of the war − we heard that President

Roosevelt had just died, and we wondered what this would mean for the future, and who would now be ruling America and making decisions affecting all of us.

It all happened so quickly — they couldn't stop as they were letting nothing hold them up in their advance. We were left chattering and speculating while they raced off.

Fairly soon the second line of the unit was upon us. This time we were taken completely in charge. They took us back to the town, and ordered that a couple of big houses be emptied. I have no idea what happened to the German families who were thus summarily turned out of their homes. We had one house for the men patients and one for the women. Most memorable of all — we were given some clothes. A great pile of various spare bits of American clothing was laid before us and we were told to take whatever we needed. We all picked out what we liked and soon most of us were in American battledress and trousers, warm and adequately clad for the first time in what seemed a very long while.

This was liberation. We were free. But it was very different from the way we had imagined it might be, during all the years of waiting and working and hoping.

The Americans were highly organised and took things over efficiently. We only stayed in the town briefly. The fighting was still going on as the allies sped to the heart of Germany. Some American lorries arrived for us, and took us back to the original camp we had left some months before. They also took complete charge of all the patients, and thus relieved me of my responsibility for them as nurse in charge.

The prisoner-of-war camps had also been bombed and several of the women there had been wounded. I met up with Ada and Krysta again. Now we were no longer prisoners of war but freed Polish forces under the protection of the Americans in an occupied and almost completely conquered Germany. A curious time of limbo now awaited us.

We didn't have to stay long in the grim surroundings of the all-too-familiar camp. The Americans had captured a factory which had been making V-1 bombs — the Germans' secret weapon with which they had bombarded Britain's southern towns. This building was given to us as our new temporary home. We moved in. But were we free? American guards were put in charge of the building and organised the administration. We could go down into the town if we wanted — but we had to get a pass every time we did so. We were told we should not travel on the public transport that was now being re-established there, nor should we get bicycles for ourselves. We were free — but not free. We tried to recognise that some of this was for our own protection: we faced the risks of rape or attack from various mobs in a countryside with no formal administration. Yet it was hard not to resent fresh rules and restrictions.

The American attitude to us was, however, extremely friendly. Every American soldier, it seemed, wanted to flirt with us and talk to us through the camp gates and give us presents. One young soldier of Italian extraction became friendly with me. We were able to talk because by now I could understand Italian through the weeks of working with the Italian doctors and orderlies. The young American, good-looking and ardent, showered me with compliments and behaved with impeccable courtesy and charm. He obtained official permission to visit me and we went for walks around the garden area that surrounded the factory. Spring was now here and trees and flowers were in bloom. Suddenly all of us Polish girls were beginning to feel that we were dignified human beings again and not just helpless degraded prisoners.

We longed to be active, and there was a great need to fill what was still an anxious time for us all, full of uncertainties about the future. The choir that had been formed during the grim early days of our imprisonment now expanded and altered to form a major part of our new lifestyle. The Americans put trucks at our disposal so that we could travel around to the many different camps of Poles (mostly displaced persons and not soldiers) and offer a full programme of community entertainment. Through our music we could express our exuberance.

There were civilian as well as military Poles in centres all over Germany — concentration camp victims, and people who had been used for forced labour, together with our airmen and soldiers captured on the different battlefronts.

With the American Army cheerfully providing transport and food, we produced concert after concert, singing and dancing and offering a taste of home.

I remember one young American soldier on one of these truck journeys sitting next to me and telling me about his Polish grandmother and how she had taught him a few Polish words including the Lord's Prayer. Rumbling across occupied and ruined Germany, we recited this most familiar and beloved of prayers. His halting words were in his strange accent. This odd little memory remains vivid in my mind.

Then came the excitement of a note from Janek telling me that he was on his way to me, hitching a lift from whatever transport was available. He had traced me with the help of the Americans. We would soon be together.

What a joy it was to see him! He was accompanied by Valery. Tracing our various movements during the months since capitulation, we found that Janek had arrived at my first prison-camp shortly after I had departed. So he had been following me more or less around Germany, although neither of us had known it. In Sandbostel, after I had left, conditions had worsened, and many people starved. Janek had seen terrible things, including even cannibalism, among the Soviet prisoners-of-war, who were the worst treated. And he himself had very nearly died of starvation, saved only by Dr Jan in the camp hospital.

A general international word for hitch-hiking – 'auto-stop' – now became a standard part of our vocabulary, and our lives. As I was no longer working as a nurse, I was busy full-time with the business of helping to co-ordinate our entertainment teams and ensuring that all the girls were trained and rehearsed. We were now running shows for American troops as well as for the Displaced Persons camps and for our own Polish military people. Janek and Valery now automatically joined me on our trips. It was so marvellous to be together, and in the rush of hurrying to the next engagement, negotiating with the Americans, organising travel and putting together shows, the haunting questions about the fate of Poland and the cause for which we had been fighting for so many years could be pushed to the back of the mind for a little while.

Chapter Fifteen

When we came back from one particular concert, I found a message waiting for me. Some one from the Polish 2nd Corps, based in Italy, had been looking for me, and had said that he would be back again in a few days. I was puzzled. I was also told that he was the adjutant of General Duch who was in command of the 3rd Carpathian Division and had been sent to look for the General's niece, Danusia. She had been in the Warsaw Rising and was known to be a prisoner of war in one of the camps.

When he arrived a couple of days later, he turned out to be none other than Jurek, an old schoolfriend of Janek's. They greeted each other enthusiastically and exchanged news. He had often been a visitor at our home in Warsaw and was a young man of great poise and charm. It felt strange to be meeting up again in Germany and in such circumstances. He had brought with him the General's niece and three of her friends from the camp at Oberlangen where he had found them. We talked and talked. Jurek was offering to taken Janek back with him to Italy, but Janek refused unless I could come too. We were determined to stick together. Eventually we found two officers from the Polish 1st Corps[1] — who had seen fighting in Belgium as part of the invasion forces — who needed to visit the 2nd Corps on official business and they agreed to take me along as an extra passenger on their jeep. This was illegal — a jeep officially took four passengers and these two officers and their two soldiers already filled it. I would make a fifth. We would have to do something to cover this when we arrived at the Italian frontier.

We made quite a group in all — Janek and Valery, Jurek,

Danusia, her three friends, and Monika, another girl from my camp: three carloads in all. It was the end of a chapter to leave Germany. I was still, of course, dressed in odd bits of American uniform, and despite my best efforts was not always a very elegant sight. One of my prize possessions was a vast American army greatcoat, which would prove to be useful on our journey across the Alps.

First I had to obtain a pass – which I still have somewhere – from the commandant of our Polish camp, authorising me to leave. When I had this I joined the others in the jeep with our bits and pieces of luggage and we headed off. The authorities were now tightening all frontier controls. So determined was I to be with my brother that nothing else seemed to matter, and I was more than prepared to take the risk of an illegal crossing. Janek and I still knew nothing about the fate of the rest of our family, and sticking together to salvage what we could of our past and build something for the future was a priority.

At Brenner on the frontier I was hidden by the simple procedure of ducking down in the jeep and being covered by a couple of blankets. No one inspected the vehicle very thoroughly. Passes and conversation were exchanged, the men's papers were checked, and we were on our way again. I was safely into Italy, albeit illegally, and the next stop would be our Polish forces. As we drove further south the climate became noticeably warmer. I no longer needed the heavy American greatcoat. The hot sun and the unfamiliar scenery, the flavour of the Mediterranean landscape, and the visibly different way of life from that of middle and eastern Europe all offered new hope, excitement and encouragement.

We reported to the headquarters of the 3rd Carpathian Division, and our credentials were accepted by the General, who was delighted to have his niece in safety. No one asked, and no one was told, how I crossed the frontier without due authorisation. All I had was a pass which gave me temporary permission to leave the Polish camp in Germany. We became guests of the officers' mess. They found rooms for us in local houses. Together with Monika I was given a room in a house belonging to two Italian ladies and their brother. They were charming and we quickly became friends. They worked as dressmakers. The Americans had presented all the Polish former prisoners in Germany with lengths of material from German factories to make clothes and my two Italian ladies now worked to create a really nice skirt and jacket, a lovely blouse made of parachute silk, and a beautiful dressing gown. The only clothing problem which remained was the delicate one of underwear − but thanks to the Italian climate I was able to wash through what I had and have it dry in under an hour, an improvement on how things had been in Germany. And, joy of joys, the Army medical supplies included something with which to treat the nits in my hair. The relief was indescribable.

The first few days were spent dealing with formalities. They had to check on my identity and I had to go to the appropriate department of our Army authorities and have my nursing diploma verified. This involved passing a special examination according to the military rules. The questions covered the whole range of my expected nursing knowledge. Then I was told I would be appointed to the staff of a new hospital that was being opened further south. There were two big camps for displaced people who for one reason or another had ended up as refugees under the care of the Polish Army. Not all were Poles, although all claimed to be. There were people who had escaped from forced labour in the Reich or who had been in camps, the human flotsam and jetsam of a vast war across Europe. There were men and women with many children and many arrivals of new babies. I started on an infectious diseases ward and then since my speciality was children's nursing, I was appointed sister-in-charge of the new children's and babies' ward.

Our questioning with the Army authorities also included a full de-briefing on the Warsaw Rising. This meant that in a very short time the word spread that we girls had been there. People were soon asking us about it with a desperate hunger for news and information about the fate of their capital city, their families and friends.

Monika would go to work with me in the hospital, but the other girls were younger, and so were allocated a place in the Polish school which had been established by the Army authorities. Meanwhile, before we took up our new jobs we were special guests in the Mess. We sat at the top table, in the 'basilica' as it was called, with the General, and the colonels and majors, watched by the younger officers in another room.

The younger officers were furious that five newly-arrived girls should be sitting only with the colonels and the majors. The General forgot to introduce us properly and so people did not know who we were. An air of mystery surrounded us. We were an object of much curiosity.

This proved mildly embarrassing. One colonel in the Mess ticked me off for not wearing proper uniform. What did I think I was doing, going about in odd bits of American clothing? I found it hard not to laugh as I explained our story. In all the years I had served in Poland's army – in secret and then in the Rising, in prison-camp, in a German forest with other bomb-victims, I had never known the luxury of a uniform, except for the white and red armbands of the AK in Warsaw. I knew by this time that I would shortly be going to work in the hospital and that I would have a full range of uniforms. In the meantime I had to cover myself with what I had!

In fact I had to borrow the money – against my first month's salary – to get my uniforms: white ones for work in the hospital and the standard officers' uniform for everyday wear.

The atmosphere in this new community was strange. Many of the men we now met had escaped from Poland after the capitulation in 1939, been interned in Hungary or Rumania, and then escaped again to France and gone from there to Britain. Others, the majority, had been deported to Russia when the Soviets invaded Eastern Poland in 1939 and had spent bitter years in prisons and forced labour in the Gulags. They had only got out when the German invasion of the USSR forced Stalin to agree to the formation of a Polish army under General Anders (who was himself a prisoner in Moscow's notorious Lubianka jail) thus enabling Poles to gather under this banner and be allowed out to fight afresh. Their mood, after subsequent years fighting in the Allied cause, was now bitter and cynical, masked by a great jollity and lots of silly jokes. They were survivors of the victory at Monte Cassino, where the most important Benedictine monastery in Europe had been destroyed in days of savage fighting. Hundreds of Poles had died there. The cynicism among members of the 2nd Corps was understandable. They knew the news from our homeland. It was now being given over to the Soviet army. For all the soft talk about the Soviets being allies of the Americans and the British, there could be no disguising what was going on.

Opinion divided about what might happen next. Few really believed that the Soviets would draw back, allow free elections or welcome our Polish government home from its wartime base in London to its rightful place on Polish soil. Some did hope that Britain and America might put pressure on the Soviets to behave decently, to negotiate, talk and compromise, opening the way for a hopeful future. Others speculated wildly about the Western Allies openly declaring war on Russia and moving in to free our country so that its own people could claim what was rightfully theirs. After all, hadn't the whole war started because of Poland? Weren't we entitled to decide our own country's future?

After months without news in the prison camps, we now had access to information. Unfortunately the news was not all welcome. It was confusing, frightening and frustrating to hear about our country's future being discussed with Stalin while his armies were encamped on our soil and showed no sign of budging. I now learned about the great meeting that had taken place in February at Yalta on the Crimea between Churchill, Stalin, and the then ailing President Roosevelt. At this conference it had been apparently agreed that a large section of the Eastern part of Poland would be handed over permanently to the USSR and that in return Poland would be given territory in the west – large tracts of land from which all the Germans would be expelled.

The Soviets had meanwhile promoted and supported a government of their own choosing – the 'Lublin Committee' – for our country, and despite British pleas that free elections should be held it seemed highly unlikely that they ever would be. At Yalta it had been officially agreed that a 'strong, free, independent and democratic' Poland should emerge. But it seemed clear that there was very little evidence of the Soviets seeking to give any substance to the words. Their ideas for the country, indeed, were far more likely to be in tune with what the Nazis had wanted — a submissive populace controlled by a secret police backed up by the grim reality of slave-labour camps. The USSR had been our immediate neighbour throughout Poland's independent life, and had invaded our country on the outbreak of war. Two-thirds of the men of the 2nd Corps had been prisoners in the Soviet labour camps and prisons and knew only too well what Soviet rule really meant.

Soon after this we learnt that some British Members of Parliament expressed their grave distrust of the Soviet Union and their fear for Poland's future when Mr Churchill reported back to them. For those of us who had fought for Poland but who were without power or influence (although not without a deep and passionate concern about what was to become of our homes, families, future and identity), the issue was not one that was going to go away.

Hearing that I had come from Poland — which most of the men of the 2nd Corps had not seen since 1939 — everyone bombarded me with questions whenever they could. Again and again I would be asked for news of relatives and friends: did I know so-and-so? Had I heard of such-and-such a family? Sadly, I was unable to help most of them: Poland was a big and well-populated country and the chances of my having knowledge of their families and acquaintances was slim.

The Warsaw Rising and the battle for the capital city had been a news item carried to them in tantalising snatches by radio or in newspapers; it had been the focus of their talk and speculation while on other battlefronts. Now they had a chance to learn it all at first hand. It bridged a gulf between us and our talk helped to forge a common understanding of our situation and destiny.

Once people came to learn who we were, I found more and more pressure to tell and re-tell the story of the Warsaw Rising. Everyone plied me with questions. I had to recount all I knew about the battle for every street, every familiar landmark or public building, every school and church and restaurant and bit of park. Everyone wanted to know what had gone on in this or that section of the city, what areas had managed to hold out to the end, which buildings might have remained intact. As to this last, I had to tell them the terrible truth: what we had seen, as we were marched around Warsaw at the end by our captors, was simply a mass of ruins. We had since heard that even these had been reduced to mere stumps or rubble by the German army moving in with bombs and hand grenades to devastate the city completely and raze it to the ground before finally retreating and leaving it to the Soviets.

It was felt that the British and the Americans had been prepared to sacrifice many Polish lives for the general Allied victories, and then to sign away Poland's own freedom in the new agreement which effectively handed over our country to Stalin. Poles, it seemed, were only good for fighting other people's battles and had no right to a homeland of their own.

All the men covered their bitterness with jokes and wry comments. Only when the talk turned to the Rising – which it did night after night once I got to know people – did the façade break. The brittle jollity would collapse and the faces would become eager and young again, the voices clamouring for this detail and that, for specific information, for named individuals – so many precious families of whom there had been no news for so long – and for day-by-day accounts of what had gone on in the different districts.

These men were battle veterans who had fought their way across half a continent and were living with the grim knowledge that their tenacity and their sacrifices, and the deaths of so many of their friends, had not won for their country its right to be free.

Having to retell my story each night was a cathartic experience for me; part of the process which eventually helped me to come to terms with the reality of what had happened. However, it would be many years before I would come to recognise that the Warsaw Rising was an inescapable part of my life, something from which I would never be released, something which like everything else simply had to be given to God.

After talking and talking late into the night, we would

sometimes turn to music, and I would sing for them the songs that had come to be part of the underground movement and the Rising. Some were already familiar to my listeners, others not. These songs brought a sense of unity with those who had fought in the Rising: those who had died and those of us who had survived to bring the news to this gathering of exiles.

At the same time as I was nightly retelling the Warsaw Rising story to my fellow Poles, I began to realise that Italy was a land of sunshine, of good wine and wonderful scenery. For the first time in years, we could enjoy decent food in pleasant restaurants. Almost every restaurant had a band which would not only play all the latest tunes but was also happy to play Polish ones to give us a flavour of home.

The war was ending. I was still a guest of the mess and had not yet taken up the new post when we got the news about the Hiroshima bomb and the final surrender of Japan. The idea of the atomic bomb was outside anything we could comprehend.

The abrupt end of the war made us examine the question of our future for the first time. Where would we go now, what would we do? It was a question facing every Pole in Italy.

We now knew there had been a ruthless carving up of Europe. This not only left Poland wholly in the Soviet camp but had denied the Western armies the prize of Berlin with all that this implied. Those eager Americans I had met in the woods outside Nordhausen had seemed unstoppable and were certainly second to none in their determination and ability to reach their goal. But now we saw what had happened: they had been forced, on the orders of their own commanders receiving directions from Allied leaders, to halt their advance. They had stopped while Berlin was almost within their grasp − and had to sit and fume while the Soviets took the city instead. The final victory of the Soviets after bitter hand-to-hand fighting with the city's inhabitants had then given way to an uneasy four-power agreement in which the former capital of the Reich was sectioned up between the USSR, America, France, and Britain. Somehow this was not the image we had all had in our minds when, in Poland, we had longed and worked for an Allied victory.

The Soviets were beginning to assert themselves as the proud masters of a new empire. In much of the continent of Europe they would replace the Nazis. The flags and banners might be different — but for the victims the misery was to be much the same. Stalin, whom many Western leaders seemed to regard with the mixture of admiration and fear which Hitler had once inspired, was the leader. It was all beginning to feel sickeningly familiar.

It was as if the Western allies had suddenly got tired, and given up, just when the last ounce of strength was needed, not for a military effort — that had been done bravely and well in the territories they had reached — but for a diplomatic and political one that would really ensure a 'just and lasting peace for all'.

Shortly after the official declaration of the end of the war, I got a letter from a friend of one of my sisters. It came as a complete surprise — but all across Europe people were contacting one another with scraps of news about friends and family. Complete strangers passed on what information they could. This girl was working as a nurse at a hospital in England, having escaped from Poland back in the 1939 fighting. I don't know how she found out where I was, but her letter was a joy. She wrote to say that my mother had been in touch with her, seeking news of me. Mother was alive and surviving on the outskirts of Warsaw. She wrote that my sisters and their children were still all right, as was Helena, Janek's wife, and Eva, his little girl.

I cannot convey what it meant to find out that Mother still lived, and to feel that one day I might see her again. The deep-rooted anxiety about my family had become so much a part of me that I had almost forgotten what it felt like to be without it. Now the relief was like a resurgence of new life. I lost no time in writing to her, sending the letter back via the girl in England, since at that time a letter from a member of the Polish forces in Italy would not necessarily have reached someone in Soviet-occupied Warsaw. Indeed it might have spelt danger to them if it had. In my letter, I could not, in any case, tell my mother where I was, as military censorship still prevailed.

From everything that we were beginning to hear, and

from the guarded tone of my mother's own letters when they began to arrive (all of them via Britain), we knew that our membership of the AK was making our families objects of suspicion to the Soviet invaders. It was better to ensure that one wrote or sent nothing incriminating. Fortunately I was able to organise the sending of regular parcels, which I would continue to mail to Warsaw during the whole of my time in Italy, using up most of my salary to try to get vital goods home to my family.

Much later I was to discover that none of these parcels ever arrived. Most had gone astray or had been pilfered along the way by people working in the various postal services.

We were shortly to learn that the AK was being dubbed 'pro-Nazi' by the Soviet leaders, and in due course some of the AK commanders would even by put on trial in Moscow and after torture and false accusations would be executed or given lengthy prison sentences so that they disappeared into the frozen wastes of the Gulag in Siberia.

Almost daily, the news from Poland was getting more bleak. What made things worse was the total lack of any understanding of the situation on the part of the British.

'What are they doing to us?' It was impossible to achieve anything by our endless anguished discussions but we could not remain silent while our country – with our homes and families in it – was handed over arbitrarily to a new enemy with the agreement of people on whose help and support we had been counting for six long years of war. 'Surely it won't really happen. They can't do this. They're just being naive and not standing up to the Soviets. It won't go on like this. Something is going to change . . . ' The arguments raged on and on – pointless, exhausting, exasperating. No one was prepared to listen to us in any case. Poles were now a minority group lost somewhere in the Allied cause, speaking in a strange Slavonic language about territory which most British people had never visited and couldn't pronounce, in a part of Europe remote from them. How much easier to be Dutch, or Belgian, or French, to belong to a nation identifiable to the British, with simple images conjured up from holidays and travel brochures: windmills, clogs, tulips, Brussels lace, Paris fashions or the Eiffel Tower! No one was suggesting that any of these Western European countries lose any territory or be subjected to Stalin's doctrinaire rules about their forms of government or the rights of their people.

I felt sick at heart whenever I went late to bed after one of these discussions. The full implications of our defeat at the hands of the Germans and the Soviets after the Rising had sunk in. For the first time since the beginning of the war I found myself looking at the future starkly with a mind shorn of any hope in any immediate enterprise. It was like looking into a void. For so long we had been saying 'When we finally get to grips with the Germans' — during those long years of struggle and waiting in Warsaw — or 'When help comes' in the Rising, or 'When the Allies reach us' in prison-camp. Now there was nothing but the stark reality of the Soviet occupation of my homeland. The grim truth to be faced was that all our struggles and disasters, death and bravery, seemed to have been in vain.

We had not faced the daily sight of round-ups or executions, the knowledge of grim consequences of discovery in the Resistance, and the final valiant stand in Warsaw simply to have the remnants of everything we cherished pass out of our grasp into the greedy hands of the Soviets. We had not honoured our country's wonderful history, its songs and its folklore, its proud heritage and its ancient Christian faith, to see these handed over to rulers whose creed was based on open affirmations of atheism.

For the first time, I began seriously to question the meaning of my Christian faith. God no longer seemed to be the loving Heavenly Father in whom I had so trustingly confided. What did it mean to be in communion with Him when He despised your poor efforts for your country so blatantly? Had we asked for something impossible from Him, in seeking to retain our independent country, based as it was largely on a Christian traditional way of life? How was it that the British and the French — neither nation noticeably more committed to Christ than the Polish — were to retain their freedom and prosperity while we were denied ours?

Against black despair everyone struggles in vain. It becomes a personal pilgrimage that you make with your Creator. No one can lead you back to God, although various

people may help you and guide you along the way. You
have to let Him do the leading. And you have to rediscover
the great truth, the great reality and message of the Cross.
Christ suffered through and for man's sins — and since that
time on Calvary no Christian has ever needed to suffer
alone. Nor has any injustice, however bitter, been wholly
without meaning — for Christ was the ultimate victim, and
He still lives.

I found that at the very darkest times, God reaches out
to you. Something of the strength imparted by Christ to
those who have tried to trust in Him is there to sustain and
uphold — even when you almost don't want it to do so.

For the Christian, there is solid comfort in the knowledge
that God is the final judge of all our actions. Every
individual — every Nazi thug and Soviet torturer, every
terrified refugee or indifferent bystander, the confused, the
gloating, the miserable, the destitute — will have to meet
His glance and receive His verdict. He sees and understands
all — especially all the parts of our lives we would rather He
didn't see.

I can only say that it was in this confused and lonely
time that I really discovered in a wholly new way what it
meant to be a Christian. You have to come to the foot of
the Cross and start all over again. Only when I had done
this — very reluctantly and with much faltering along the
way — did anything begin to make sense. Christianity took
on a different dimension and a new meaning.

NOTES

Chapter 15

1. It is interesting to note that it was this Polish First Corps which
   liberated the prisoner-of-war camp at Oberlangen. They had
   been amazed to find it full of young Polish girls. The Corps
   had been fighting its way across Germany with the Allied
   invasion force.

Chapter Sixteen

As a small group of girls among so many men, it is not surprising that we were surrounded by dozens of suitors. Every young officer seemed to see in us a symbol of home, an opportunity to express all their ideas of chivalry and honour, love and gallantry for which there had been no time during the fighting. 'Mother would have wanted me to marry a girl like you' was the unspoken comment in dozens of pairs of eyes. At every social event we were surrounded by young men eager for our attention.

Nonetheless, there was something of a gulf between those of us who had endured the Occupation in Poland or been deported to Russia, and those who had been in the West during those fateful years. We felt that the last group was out of touch with the reality of what had been happening in our homeland. Coming as they did from Britain, where, whatever their tales of bombing and food rationing, a normal life had been possible, what could they know of what we had endured? Their lives had not been dull, but their stomachs had been full. To them, the Gestapo had been a distant enemy across an ocean barrier.

In answer to questions I tried to convey the terror that accompanied a round-up in the street, or the stark horror of lists of names on an execution announcement, but it was not easy. They were not deliberately ignorant – everyone did their best to feel a sense of identity with those who had remained behind – but they simply could not be expected to understand fully.

In the early Autumn of 1945, I left the headquarters of the Division to go to the South of Italy to work as a sister in the new hospital there: Polish Military Hospital Number 340 in Trani. Here I started, virtually from scratch, the children's and babies' ward which was essential for the growing Polish civilian population in the two camps, Trani and Barletta. The British authorities had provided the basic necessities for the military hospital and its staff but I had to acquire all the things that the children and babies would need such as little pyjamas and makeshift cots.

I put Monika in charge of the children's diet and food. We all had problems with the British system of measurements, having been brought up on the metric system. I had a busy time training the nurses — who had been used only to caring for military wounded and sick — in the treatment of children. I had to explain how to give injections and drips, and how to administer medicines.

Many of the children were suffering from pneumonia and dysentery — because of the change of climate and the lack of care and knowledge on the part of the mothers. I had charge of ten nurses, twelve auxiliaries (young girls who were given simple cleaning and routine tasks to do), two orderlies, and between 15 and 20 mothers whose babies were our patients and who stayed with us because they were breast-feeding them. We were fortunate in having an excellent and gifted consultant, Dr Kapelner, a specialist paediatrician for whom no patient was too much trouble and who gave superb care.

Janek meanwhile had joined his reconstituted regiment of the 7th Lancers which had been operating as *Jelen* in the underground and of course he and I kept in regular contact while I was in Trani. In the spring I was invited back to the regimental headquarters for the annual festival on 23rd March — commemoration of the decoration of our regimental standard with the Virtuti Militari Cross in 1921 by Marshall Pilsudski after the war against the Bolsheviks. There was a special Mass and march-past and a ceremony in which a number of us were formally given our regimental badges by the Colonel. After this we were presented to the commander-in-chief of the Polish forces, General Anders, and there was a formal dinner for the whole regiment, at long tables set out in the open air. There was a pageant depicting the history of the regiment, followed by speeches and toasts and during the day there was also a football match and all kinds of other entertainments and celebrations.

It was perhaps inevitable that I was going to marry one of the young officers of the Carpathian division in Italy, and that is what I did. A young man had been staring and staring at me while I sat in the 'basilica' of the mess, and when we finally got talking I found he was Slawek Wolkowinski, an old school friend of Janek's, who had recognised me from long ago in Warsaw. Here at last was a link with home, with my mother and sisters and the days when I was a little girl. I remembered Slawek visiting us first as a boy in his school uniform and then later as a university student while I was still a schoolgirl. He was then interested in my older sister rather than me! Now the years had rolled by and we had both had so many adventures. He had escaped from Poland into Hungary with his unit on the outbreak of war and been interned there. Later he escaped again to rejoin the Polish Army and saw action in the Middle East, Africa, Tobruk and Italy including Bologna and Monte Cassino. Now we were meeting and talking here in the Italian sunshine ... He told me he had finished his law diploma in Warsaw in the spring of 1939, following in the tradition of his father and grandfather who had both been lawyers. We began to spend our leisure time together. We visited Rome, and the ruins of Monte Cassino. In Rome, we went to St Pauls-outside-the-walls at sunset, when the sun gleamed through the windows which are not of glass but of translucent marble. It was almost unbearably beautiful.

I finally accepted his proposal on Christmas Eve of 1945 and we celebrated our engagement with a party on New Year's Eve.

It began as a private party, and then moved on to the 7th Lancers Mess. There, Slawek was subjected to a lot of teasing because the Lancer officers felt indignant that I was marrying out of the regiment, and not even a cavalry officer. He had to consume a huge amount of drink, forbidden to refuse anything. After the Mess, things moved on to yet another party at a nearby club. At one point twelve of us were on the same jeep, hurtling on to the next round of drinks. It was the early hours of the morning, and dawn was breaking, when things finally drew to a reluctant close.

Our wedding was in July 1946. It was now more than a year after the war's end and we had all become a fairly established community of Poles in Italy. The wedding was a family occasion — Janek had succeeded in getting Helena and little Eva safely out of Poland after a hair-raising journey and they arrived just 24 hours before the wedding, to start a new life as I was starting mine. They brought news from home, and I was able to know that my mother knew about my marriage and was wishing me well and praying for me.

We had decided to marry in Rome. On the wedding morning, there was a Mass in the Crypt of St Paul's-outside-the-walls and then the wedding ceremony took place in the Polish church at noon. Father Joniec, chief chaplain to the 3rd Division, officiated. According to Polish custom, the bride is accompanied to the church by two young men, and the bridegroom by two young girls. Also, before the bride leaves for the church, she receives her parents' blessing. Janek came for me in an open army car accompanied by his colonel. I was waiting in my white silk bridal outfit, clutching my bouquet of orange-blossoms. As my mother was not able to be present, Janek gave me the traditional blessing, tracing the sign of the Cross on my forehead. Then we went out to the car, while a friendly crowd gathered to clap and cheer as we set off. Slawek joined us at the church with Helena and Eva taking the role of his traditional attendants. It was a beautiful wedding and the reception afterwards was at a nearby restaurant, under sun-dappled vine leaves. We had had to arrange everything ourselves, as of course neither of us had parents present. Indeed, Slawek had no one from his family at all at his wedding. As he was Orthodox, I had had to receive special permission from the Catholic Church to marry him, both of us agreeing to bring the children up as Catholics.

We spent our honeymoon touring Italy and then Slawek came back with me to Trani for a few days as I had to return to duty and he still had a week's more leave.

Of course our thoughts were now all focused on the future. We had to make plans and face difficult choices. We were now all getting news and information from different sources and contacts. I heard from an aunt in America about the particular dangers awaiting AK members who ventured back to Warsaw.

The British now began to apply their own logic to our problems. We started to hear rumours that we might all be forcibly sent back to Poland – repatriated against our will to face certain death or imprisonment. That this was not an empty threat we were to have confirmed many years later when we learned about the full details of the Yugoslav and Russian emigré repatriations by the Allies, and their aftermath of death in the Gulag. However, the British drew back from implementing the policy with regard to us. They did their best to persuade us, cajoling and arguing, but they stopped short of using force. This saved our lives – the fate of AK members in Stalin's Poland was grim.[1]

Eventually we were offered another option: the chance of settling in Great Britain.

I could never have imagined that there would be a time when, married to a Polish officer and myself proudly wearing my country's uniform, I could make the decision to share a new life not in the land of our birth and upbringing but in distant England. But the Poland for which we had all been fighting, the free homeland of our own that had been the simple hope of all those years of struggle, had now been taken over by brutal rulers and we could not return as tenants to these particular landlords.

Nor could we impose risks on our families who without us might just manage to survive but with our arrival would find themselves subjected to the prospect of a labour camp. Appalling as it was to recognise the fact, we had to see that if we tried to return home we would be a danger to those we loved.

The priest who officiated at our wedding, the Polish forces chaplain, did return to Poland. He was asked to do so by his bishop and felt he should not refuse. However, as we learned much later, on arrival he had to go into hiding, and later died in an obscure village.

We bore no ill-will towards the English we met in Italy. John, the British liaison officer to our regiment, became a good friend and would later attend the christening of our first child in England. They simply couldn't understand our sorrowing or our dilemma. As far as we could see, the British disliked and distrusted the Soviets, and would have fought every inch of the way had it been London and not Warsaw which was to have a puppet government imposed upon it with the USSR pulling the strings — but they just couldn't understand that Poles felt exactly the same. Nor would they recognise that we already knew quite a lot about Soviet power and methods, that the USSR had tried to annexe our country a generation earlier, in the 1920s, and that since the invasion of 17th September 1939 large numbers of Polish people — including many of our own friends and relatives — had disappeared without trace into the dark void of Stalin's prison empire.

It seemed to us that while ordinary British people knew little of Poland or indeed of central European history as a whole, their government (together with those of other Western Allied countries) was prepared to hand over this territory to the Soviets in return for an uneasy peace. In doing this, they were handing over independent sovereign states to a new empire which had no right to them. Everything, it seemed, had to be done to appease 'Uncle' Joe Stalin.

We admired Britain for her stand against Hitler, and believed that some day she might be a moral force against other evil dictators too. We wanted to co-operate with the British people and to fulfil a useful and loyal role in British society. However, the gulf between the British and the Polish way of looking at things emerged when we were questioned prior to our settlement being arranged. The pleasant, correctly-mannered official in charge of our interrogation could not understand my reluctance to give the full names and addresses of all my known relatives living in Poland.

'Can you guarantee that you won't pass these names on to the Soviets?' I asked hesitantly through the interpreter, who stood translating my words into this strange clipped language that one day, soon, I too would be learning to speak. Back came the response — no, such a guarantee could not be given. The Soviets had, after all, been the official allies of the British for the last four years of the war. 'Then I'm afraid I can't give you the names − I'm so sorry.' I hoped my voice didn't show my fear; in any case I wasn't going to budge on this. Polite, and sometimes not so polite, attempts to reassure, charm and wheedle, were ineffective: when your family's safety is at stake you don't give in. The British faced a similar stubbornness among all the newly-exiled Poles. Eventually, we were admitted for settlement in any case. We knew we had no job prospects, no home and (in my own case) no knowledge of the language or customs, but we had nowhere else to go, and we were grateful for a place where we could live in freedom. Slawek at least had the advantage that he spoke many languages fluently including English.

Poland had lost six million people − almost one in five of our population. We had lost the best of our generation: slaughtered by the Soviets at Katyn, killed in the German concentration camps, slain in battle at Monte Cassino, or dead in the ruins of Warsaw. And we had nothing to show for all the loss, misery and devastation. We could not say, as the British were now saying of their own war dead: 'They did not die in vain − our country is still free.'

The winter of 1946 was the most bitter one in living memory. The crossing to England was a difficult one. We were kept waiting two days in Calais because the Channel was too rough for any ship, and when we finally sailed everyone was seasick.

England was a country we knew only from history books. We were placed in a resettlement camp and tried to turn our faces to the future. The icy cold struck not only into our bones but into our hearts.

Some of the older people could not believe that this exile would last − they kept their cases packed under their bunks in the freezing barracks, convincing themselves that they might yet go home. But it was not to be. We all had to face a long winter of suffering and waiting, and then many springtimes of work, struggle, and hope, before the summer would come again for us and for Poland.

NOTES

Chapter 16

1. There are many examples. Here is one: Richard Pape, whose escape as an RAF prisoner-of-war and assistance to the Polish underground is vividly described in his book *Boldness be my Friend*, tells how Mietek, a Pole who had befriended him and rendered invaluable service to the Allied cause, was treated. Arrested in Lvov where he and others fought alongside the Russians to liberate the city from the Nazis, Mietek was imprisoned in the notorious Kolyma region, forced to work in the gold-mines, and returned after twelve long years minus one eye, partially paralysed, and unable to walk properly because of frostbite.

Alexander Solzenhitsyn also records in his *Gulag Archipelago*, that there were a number of Poles who had been in the Home Army in the death-camps of Kolyma during the late 1940s and early 50s. Many of these will be among the millions of dead whose bodies lie beneath the permafrost of that remote region.

Sir Winston Churchill recalls in his official account of the Second World War: 'At the beginning of March 1945 the Polish Underground was invited by the Russian Political Police to send a delegation to Moscow to discuss the formation of a united Polish Government along the lines of the Yalta agreement. This was followed by a written guarantee of personal safety, and it was understood that the party would later to allowed, if the negotiations were successful, to travel to London for talks with the Polish Government in exile. On March 27 General Leopold Okulicki, the successor of General Bor-Komorowski in command of the Underground Army, two other leaders, and an interpreter had a meeting in the suburbs of Warsaw with a Soviet representative. They were joined the following day by eleven leaders representing the major political parties in Poland. One other Polish leader was already in Russian hands. No one returned from the rendezvous. On April 6 the Polish Government in exile issued a statement in London giving the outline of this sinister episode. The most valuable representatives of the Polish Underground had disappeared without a trace in spite of the formal Russian offer of safe-conduct. Questions were asked in Parliament, and stories have since spread of the shooting of local Polish leaders in the areas at this time occupied by the Soviet armies, and particularly of one episode at Siedlce, in Eastern Poland. It was not until May 4 that Molotov admitted at San Francisco that these men were being held in Russia, and an official Russian news agency stated next day that they were awaiting trial on charges of 'diversionary tactics in the rear of the Red Army'.

On May 18 Stalin publicly denied that the arrested Polish leaders had ever been invited to Moscow, and asserted that they were mere 'diversionists' who would be dealt with according to 'a law similar to the British Defence of the Realm Act'. The Soviet Government refused to move from this position. Nothing more was heard of the victims of the trap until the case against them opened on June 18. It was conducted in the usual Communist manner. The prisoners were accused of subversion, terrorism, and espionage, and all except one admitted wholly or in part the charges against them. Thirteen were found guilty, and sentenced to terms of imprisonment ranging from four months to ten years, and three were acquitted. This was in fact the judicial liquidation of the leadership of the Polish Underground which had fought so heroically against Hitler. The rank and file had already died in the ruins of Warsaw.'

Postscript

One day Slawek received a message from General Kopanski, who had been his commanding officer in the Africa campaigns and was now on the headquarters staff. He told Slawek that the Soviets had prepared a list of people they were demanding should be deported to the USSR. They were claiming they were deserters from the Red Army. Slawek's name was on the list because he had been born in Charkov in Russia − and as his surname began with a W, which is near the front of the Russian alphabet, his name was at the top of the list. Because the general knew Slawek well, he was able to tell the British authorities that this Soviet list was nonsense and that it consisted merely of people whose place of birth happened to be within the old Russian borders. We knew that to return to Poland with this deportation order hanging over us added to the dangers we already faced as a result of my membership of the AK. The news of the existence of this so-called deserters list was what finally removed our thoughts of returning home. Fortunately, the General's wise handling of the subject with the British authorities stopped them from attempting to deport us. Slawek's position gave the General the proof he needed that the list was purely a Soviet invention − a method of attempting to arrest Polish officers on a trumped-up excuse.

Facing all the facts, and knowing that we must tackle our future, Slawek and I made two firm decisions. Firstly, we had to recognise that a return to Poland was not feasible. Secondly, we wanted to leave the depressing atmosphere of the camp and make our own way.

As a young newly-married couple we had had enough of

uniforms, barracks and regulations. As soon as we could do so, we left — with £200 that Slawek had saved up from his Army earnings and which we put down as a deposit on a war-damaged house in Battersea in South London. Slawek managed to get a job in a bric-a-brac shop, his university degree and Polish qualifications as a lawyer being of little use to him in this new land.

I felt trapped by being unable to speak or understand anybody. When a woman accidentally jostled against me in the Underground and muttered 'Bloody foreigner' I replied politely and tried to commit her words to memory, thinking it was some kind of useful formal phrase that I ought to learn .... Gradually my vocabulary improved, and I was finally able to get a job as a nurse and my diploma was recognised. And so a new life had begun.

The story of post-war Poles in Britain deserves its own book. Although we were dispersed all around Britain, we tried very hard to maintain contact with one another. Our Polish priests, ex-chaplains of our forces or survivors of the concentration camps, were a huge help, arranging services and encouraging us to organise ourselves into communities of mutual support and co-operation. In London, we negotiated for a weekly Sunday Mass at Brompton Oratory and this became a focal point for many families.

Children arrived, and a new chapter of our family history was being written here in exile. Our first child we named Paul, after the great writer of the Epistles, whose message about love, 'the greatest of these is love', had always meant a great deal to me. The name was also a reminder of St Paul's-outside-the-walls in Rome where the light shines through translucent marble windows and where Mass had been celebrated for us on the morning of our wedding.

Three years after Paul's birth, a brother arrived, and we decided to name him Peter after the other great Apostle. Every year the two boys thus shared a joint 'name day' on 29th June, the Feast of St Peter and Paul, and tended to complain because they didn't each have a special day of their own! Our family was completed with the arrival of our youngest son, Konrad, named after his Wolkowinski grandfather and great-grandfather.

The children gave a whole new meaning and purpose to our lives. We wanted to bring them up in our Christian faith and pass on to them a love of country and culture. Most important of all, we wanted them to grow up in freedom — settling in Britain was worth all the sacrifices just for that. But of course we also wanted them to be Polish, and to know and love their heritage.

As a Polish community, we found that this attitude did not always meet with approval or understanding from headmasters and teachers. Many tried to persuade us that being bi-lingual might give our children complexes or restrict their normal development. In the Church, too, we met many questions: why have special Masses or services in Polish? Why Polish Catholic organisations? We must have seemed very obstinate and unreasonable, but the majority of us wanted to pass on to the children certain values for which we had been prepared to die in the war and for which we were now determined to live, despite all the difficulties. Later, the attitudes changed. Fewer people said 'Why?' to us, and more began to say 'We understand'. And our children seem to have benefited, rather than suffered, by being enriched by two cultures and fluent in two languages.

I am proud of my three boys. Paul married an English girl, Lynn — they have a little son, Edward, and live in Australia. Peter married a Polish girl, Teresa, and has a family of three girls and a boy — Margaret, Natalie, Katherine, and Maximillian. They live in France. Konrad lives and works in London and now that I am getting older he is the one I can see and chat with regularly — I enjoy his company very much. It is for my thre sons and my grandchildren that I have written this book.

When the children were small we tried to maintain contact with home as far as we could without endangering our families. I sent my mother a recording of them saying their bed-time prayers in Polish. Later I discovered that the Polish authorities had played the tape round and round repeatedly, convinced that it held some secret message: when it finally reached my mother it was indecipherable.

Janek and Helena had settled, like us, in England. Janek learned a new trade and became a watch-mender. When my husband got a job as a lecturer and we moved to new homes, first in Cornwall and then in Scotland, there were happy family holidays in which all our children played together, and we formed a new extended family here in exile. We knew we were so very much more fortunate than many others.

I wrote to Hanka, to whom I had entrusted my private possessions on the day before the Warsaw Rising, and begged for the return of the thing that mattered most – the prayer book that belonged to my childhood. All communication with Poland was difficult – you never knew if letters would arrive or who would be reading them on the way. And maybe Hanka just didn't understand how much this link with the old life meant to me. I had to write again and again. It was a long while before I had the book safely, but its final arrival gave me a sort of peace.

My greatest longing – to see my mother again – was not to be fulfilled. After a good many years, during which time Slawek and I had been granted British citizenship, it proved possible to arrange for her to come and visit us in England. The paperwork and negotiations involved were considerable – both for her and for us – but at long last it did seem as though the thing I had so often dreamed of might happen. I had last seen her walking off quietly down the street, just days before the Rising, when I had been too busy to talk.

I had her room prepared, and the children were excitedly awaiting the arrival of their grandmother, when a telegram came. The tragic, the almost unbelievable, had happened – my mother was seriously ill. Telephone calls went back and forth. The news got worse. Two weeks later she was dead. There was to be no happy reunion in Britain. Numb with the news, I found this the hardest thing in my life to bear – that we had not been allowed that final time together.

In the middle 1960s, it became possible for me, now carrying a British passport, to return for a visit to Poland. I took my eldest son, Paul with me. It is impossible to convey the emotions of that trip. The Stalin years were over, and we could visit the AK graves in Warsaw's cemetery. Some of those lying there had been officially classified as criminals by the Soviets in the early post-war years and now the birchwood crosses bore the recently added words 'rehabilitated' and the date when posthumous pardon for uncommitted crimes had been granted. I found Wlodek's name on the regimental memorial for members of our unit. And I thought of all the others – Krystyna, Zbyszek, Krysztof and his wife, Jan with whom I had sang at the piano.

I went back to the pharmacy at 4 Pulawska Street, and retraced my steps along the route taken in front of the German tanks. I also visited the Old Town which I had last seen devastated, a mass of ruins. It had been lovingly rebuilt stone by stone by ordinary people, and the work was still continuing. Here I rediscovered the Warsaw I had always known. Elsewhere, things were so different: the skyline was dominated by the vast Palace of Culture which everybody hated and strange new suburbs consisting entirely of identical blocks of flats looked bleak and unfamiliar. Foodstuffs and all basic essentials seemed terribly scarce when compared with the abundance of England: but I had expected this and had brought as much as I possibly could to distribute. It was so heartbreaking to see the people of Poland so humiliated and cast down: an energetic and creative nation squeezed into the economic cul-de-sac of Marxism which wasted the fruits of their labour and robbed them of their right to enough food, decent homes, attractive clothes. The Communists had denied Poland the help from America – Marshall aid – after the war, which had given much-needed assistance to Western Europe. They kept telling people to work harder, to believe in socialism, to refrain from any comment or criticism under pain of punishment. Warsaw had echoes of the past but it lacked completely the life and vitality of the city I had known. Above all, it was a city where the truth was not being told – about world events, about current problems, about the tragic experiences twenty years earlier which had marked so many families. Ordinary people were being expected to live a lie, and knew it.

But Communism could not last for ever, and twenty years later its collapse was imminent. The most dramatic event in post-war Poland's history was the election of a Polish Pope in 1978, when Archbishop Karol Woytyla was elected in Rome. The news created an exultation and jubilation in

Poles around the world – none of us will ever forget that evening. We remember where we were when the news first broke, and what we were doing.

We all knew that this would mean that nothing could be the same in Poland. When Pope John Paul went back in triumph to his homeland he set it on fire with new hope and optimism. Millions massed to see him, and Communist officialdom melted away as towns and cities came to a standstill and the vast crowds gathered to celebrate. After this, the formation of Solidarity showed the world how the Poles were to go about changing things.

There was a sense that, at last, the tide of history was running in the right direction.

Of course the Communists tried to hang on to power. Eventually, when Solidarity, which had begun as a trade union movement in a shipyard, looked like being a serious challenge to the whole Marxist order of things, they imposed martial law. I was staying in Warsaw on another family visit when this took place and that was how, for the third time in my life, I awoke in the early hours of the morning to the sound of massive military movements in my native city: first with the invasion in '39, next in the Rising, and now this.

During the period of martial law, young people in Poland, who had all been taught about Polish history by their parents and aunts and uncles, found a renewed identification with the by now legendary AK and the underground fight against the Nazis. The old AK symbol was revived, and would be chalked on walls or hand-printed on illegal posters. There were commemorative events on the anniversary of the Rising. All of this was intensely moving to those of us who had lived through 1944.

When I saw young people gathering in Warsaw in old bits of makeshift wartime army uniform to honour the dead of the Rising, I recognised that something very precious had been passed on.

Not very much later, Communism was finally over. The Communists had to reach a compromise with Solidarity, and this led to a sharing of power, which was the first step on the road to free elections. When these finally took place, a new era had started.

Communism has left a grim legacy in Poland. The land is polluted and the economy is wrecked, with decades of 'socialist planning' accounting for wasted money, wasted resources, and abuse of men's skills and time. Hope and faith will be needed to eradicate old attitudes and build for the future. But it was this future for which people struggled and died during the Warsaw Rising.